LaoTsePress

RIDING THE HORSE BACKWARDS

A graduate of MIT and the Jung Institute of Zurich, Switzerland, **Arnold Mindell, Ph.D.**, is the founder of a new school of therapy called Process Oriented Psychology. Dr Mindell is known throughout the world for his innovative synthesis of dreams and bodywork, Jungian therapy, and group process, consciousness, shamanism, quantum phusics and small and large group conflict resolution. He is the author of 15 other books including *Dreambody, The Leader as Martial Artist, The Shaman's Body, Sitting in the Fire* and *Quantum Mind.*

Amy Mindell, Ph.D., author of *Metaskills* and *Coma, A Healing Journey,* and *Alternative to Therapy,* is a co-developer of Process Oriented Psychology and has made major contributions to the body of knowledge of Process Oriented Psychology. Along with her husband she has regularly facilitated large group sessions and town meetings around the world using the Process Work approach.

The Mindells have established Process Work training centers in 22 countries and frenquentlys appear as the keynote speakers at international professional confrences as well as on TV and radio shows in the US, Canada, England, Germany, Japan, Poland and Switzerland.

"The Foundation Series" orignially published between 1985 and 1992 includes *Working with the Dreaming Body, The Dreambody in Relationships, Riding the Horse Backwards* and *Working on Yourself Alone.* It represents some of the most exciting and formative examples of Process Oriented Psychology.

Other books by Amy Mindell
Alternative to Therapy
Coma, A Healing Journey
Metaskills

Other books by Arnold Mindell
The Deep Democracy of Open Forums: How to Transform Organizations into Communities

The Dreammaker's Apprentice

Dreaming While Awake

Quantum Mind: The Edge Between Physics and Psychology

Sitting in the Fire: Large Group Transformation Using Conflict and Diversity

The Shaman's Body: A New Shamanism for Transforming Health, Relationship, and Community

The Leader as Martial Artist: An Introduction to Deep Democracy

The Year I: Global Process Work and Planetary Tensions

Working on Yourself Alone: Inner Dreambodywork

Coma, Key to Awakening: Working with the Dreambody near Death

City Shadows: Psychological Interventions in Psychiatry

The Dreambody in Relationships

River's Way: The Process Science of the Dreambody

Working with the Dreaming Body

Dreambody: The Body's Role in Revealing the Self

Riding the Horse Backwards

ARNOLD AND AMY MINDELL

Riding the Horse Backwards

Process Work in Theory and Practice

LAO TSE PRESS
PORTLAND, OREGON

Distributed to the trade by Words Distributing Company, 7900 Edgewater Drive, Oakland, CA 94621.

First published by Arkana 1992

Printed in the United States of America

Mindell, Arnold, 1940–
Mindell, Amy, 1958

LCCN 2001095028

Contents

In the Tub

R iding the Horse Backwards is for people interested in their own personal growth and for facilitators of personal growth, and will also be of use to those interested in dance and art, group work, and transpersonal psychology. It reports emerging philosophy, methods, and applications of process-oriented psychology through transcripts and descriptions of process work in action at a seminar and at courses held during our first Esalen residency in 1987-8.

Process work, as process-oriented psychology is often called, extends the Jungian concept of the unconscious and the methods of Gestalt practice. It incorporates the feeling of shamanism and performing arts, and touches upon healing, meditation, and awareness procedures. Process work might well be categorized as one of the new transpersonal psychologies since it attempts to bring together spiritual practices with Western psychological methods.

In the first chapter Arny recounts the development of process-oriented psychology, which began in Zurich in the early 1970s as he expanded some of C.G. Jung's ideas in his need to bring movement and bodywork into his work as a Jungian analyst. It was during this period that Arny wrote *Dreambody*, in which he describes the relationship between dream images and body experiences.

Dreambody addressed a public anxious to have a psychothera-peutic approach that fills the theoretical gap between psyche and soma. Before Arny or the rest of us in Zurich realized what was happening, process work became known to many professionals all around the world. This rapid development happened, in part, because of the teaching and training we did in Europe and the United States, and also because of the worldwide need to unite the different psychologies. The growth of this work continued with the distribution of *Dreambody* and Arny's second book, *Working with the Dreaming Body*.

Soon Arny added relationship work and signal theory to dream and bodywork, and process-oriented psychology began to expand. Bodywork led him into yoga and meditation procedures, and these, in turn, inspired working with people in strongly altered states of consciousness.

Our ensuing extraordinary experiences with people near death produced *Coma: Key to Awakening*, which opened up new terri-tory in working with the dying. In that book Arny showed that people in comatose conditions were in the midst of dreaming pro-cesses and could be communicated with. Applying these ideas in working with apparently hopeless psychiatric patients resulted in the publication of *City Shadows*, a book that addresses new, non-chemical ways of working with chronic mental disturbances. *Working on Yourself Alone* extended dreambodywork to inner prac-tice and *The Year I* discussed what we call worldwork, which deals with conflict and community making.

Process-oriented psychology is itself in process, undergoing a phase of rapid change and growth. It is therefore difficult to describe its next stage of development. While Arny and I were recently in Kyoto we found ourselves explaining process work to Japanese Zen students, who, to our delight, already knew what it was about! "Nature, the Tao, oh yes," they said. They were not surprised when we said that the future of process work itself was part of the Tao. We think that if it is on the right track, then it will succeed. If it is off, that is, if it does not retain its basic flexibility, then it must disappear like other psychotherapies that contain an implicit nucleus of rigidity.

As we work with different individuals and groups around the world, we spend less time in private practice. At first we resisted leaving this one-to-one setting, which we love so much and which is the anchor for everything else we do. Later, we realized that individual work was only one part of our profession, which could also include work with conflict in large groups, and work with families.

Working with individuals, couples, and small groups in front of ever larger audiences brought Arny unexpected insights and enabled him to function even better as an individual therapist. He became upset, touched, and fascinated by the way in which people relate to one another. And from this, a new form of process work with groups and organizations emerged, using the same paradigm—follow what everyone notices and what they choose not to notice as well.

It was out experience in Africa that finally showed us the context for our work. Chance had it that we ended up in the bush with a husband and wife team of shamans. We will talk about this in greater detail in later chapters, but I must mention here that as we sat on the earth floor of a hut near Mombasa on the Indian Ocean, we realized that process work had its roots in ancient and yet ageless traditions that integrated individual and group work, personal problems and cultural renewal. Of course, we had known that from our studies in anthropology and mythology, but those beautiful shamans showed it to us. They fell on the floor, rolled over in altered states and ecstatic trances and made us feel at home. Arny said again and again, "Amy, I feel like we're home!" To tell the truth, I did not feel all that much at home. After all, I had never been healed before by people who sang, danced, prayed, and rubbed a dripping wet, live chicken over my naked body! But that is another story.

One unexpected result of our work with all sorts of people in various states was that we were enjoying ourselves more. What we were doing didn't feel like work! We began to wonder exactly what it was we were doing. Is process-oriented psychology a psychology?

If so, then psychology suddenly included all kinds of things we had never learned in school, like fun, art, and creativity. The therapeutic element remained, but larger questions emerged. What are our goals in life? What is the position of "psychological" work in cultural change? Is the psychologist a modem shaman working with the spirit of the times? And how can music, dance, healing, and just plain fun fit into our earlier psychological work?

Process work includes all of these elements. Arny had many friends, and even some critics, helping him and a group of around one hundred people in Zurich put together the first process-oriented psychology training program in the early 1980s. This was soon followed by centers in the United States, England, Australia, Africa and Asia.

The rapidly developing organization, whose direction was unknown, catapulted us into situations, cultures, and difficulties we had never encountered. From the challenge of our own growth grew the application of the process paradigm to large group situations, which we tested in different areas of the world. We worked with people who did not speak our language or share our beliefs. Off we went to Israel and Kenya, South Africa and India, Japan and southern Europe.

After our initial success at testing these concepts, we were confronted with sobering questions. We studied videotapes and saw that there were moments in which our work required greater ability, theory, and insight. We began to research our work and found that it had transpersonal goals and values, carrying on the hope and excitement begun by Perls, Rogers, Maslow, and Grof in developing methods for dealing with large groups without losing touch with spiritual values.

This work is still too young for us to have an overview of it. Perhaps we will never have the objectivity because the future of process work depends, by its very nature, upon the personal development of its practitioners and the changes in humankind all over the world. Who knows? Perhaps our work will disappear as quickly as it arose. Whatever happens, it is still young enough to be exciting and lawless. Our growth now takes us in the direction of settling down, and we are spending more time in a newly created clinic and training center in Portland and Yachats, Oregon, where we are also establishing a cross-cultural conflict resolution program.

Though we have worked in many places, with many types of people, one of the most enjoyable and challenging jobs we have had was working for Esalen. As process work became better known, members of the Esalen community came to our seminars and eventually invited us to work with them in Big Sur. The seminar described in this book was the beginning of our ongoing relationship with Esalen.

The following pages are essentially a transcript of the video-taped recording of a public seminar entitled "Introduction to Process-oriented Psychology," which Arny conducted and I assisted at the Esalen Institute, Big Sur, California. Some explanatory notes have been added from a similar seminar we gave together in the fall of 1988 for the in-house Esalen staff, the community living and working at Esalen and the surrounding area.

Arny and I have edited the material only minimally, to honor the privacy of the participants and to make the contents readable. We transcribed movement and nonverbal interactions as best we could, and I have added simple sketches of the actual work where I thought they were needed. We omitted unnecessary repetitions and tried, above all, to preserve the feeling of experiential study. We believe that this experiential aspect is as important to the development of psychology and psychosomatic medicine as is the theory of process-oriented psychology, which appears in Arny's earlier books.

We would like to take the reader into the excitement, magic, and mood of a seminar. We want this book to reveal personal and theoretical secrets that have not appeared in print elsewhere. It is an attempt to pull together our growing knowledge of the philosophy and interventions of process work in the fields of psychiatry, meditation, coma work, dream and bodywork, relationship work, art, movement, and large-group work, and, finally, to combine it all with transpersonal thinking.

***

The idea for this book arose in an Esalen hot tub one night during the weekend seminar. Arny and I were unexpectedly enlightened that evening by an unknown seminar participant sitting with us in the baths overlooking the Pacific. We could barely see his face in the darkness. Let's call him Ron.

Ron told us that he had seen Arny lecture some time ago in Zurich, but that he left the lecture early because he felt Arny was enjoying himself too much. Now, a few years later, after having been with us at Esalen, Ron felt that it was time for his own creativity to emerge, time for him to begin to enjoy his work as a psychotherapist.

Ron praised Arny for his artistry. Arny got extremely embarrassed and had difficulty accepting this public sentiment. In fact, Arny became so shy about the praise he received at the seminar that we had our first disagreement while creating this book. I wanted to leave in some of the praise at the end of the manuscript and Arny got upset. He thought the comments and compliments would make him look like a guru in the eyes of the public, while I thought they were genuine and belonged to the atmosphere of a real seminar. I argued that the way he dealt with praise was part of relationship work, and furthermore, that what we teach is who we are. If the reader wanted a more academic approach, he or she could find it elsewhere (See Bibliography). This book, though, is a personal approach to the philosophy and theory of process work. My argument worked!

Ron told us that night that he thought process work did not fit into any of the different psychotherapeutic categories. He saw Arny using dance, painting, and choreography to work with each person's issues, and he felt that it was art, not science, that led to the numinous experiences the participants had. He saw each work as a piece of art in which the most dreaded parts of people unfolded into profound meaning and power. He wondered how each work could be so unfailingly surprising, and we asked ourselves, "Where is psychology going?" We all agreed that healing was an important but limiting concept in therapy and that psychology wanted to increase its scope.

I told Ron that I was excited by process work because of its broad-spectrum approach to individuals, relationships, and groups. Ron, however, was moved by something else: its generosity and openness. He wondered how Arny and I could invite people to sit with us at lunch, to ask questions and to find out who we were. Did the sense of sacredness and religious experience come from simply valuing people?

In Ron's opinion process work was magic. He thought there could be no recipes to learn it. Obviously it was important that each person developed his own way of working, his own magic. Magic. That was what I had been trying to teach my students in Zurich, and what I had been calling my own research in process work. Magic! I meditated in the tub about writing up the seminar transcript to show how magic arises from believing that the seeds of life lie in the unexpected, indeed, in the trouble and garbage that we throw away. I hoped we could show on paper how to transform mundane reality into a wonderland.

Little did we know that this first weekend workshop at Esalen in 1987 would be the start of our residency there. Several months later we were asked to come as the first in a visiting-teacher program to "improve the quality of work at Esalen" (*See Chapter 12*). We want to thank the in-house Esalen community for the experience of teaching there and for creating the atmosphere from which this book was derived. We are also deeply indebted to all of our Esalen seminar participants and especially to those whose work is reported here for their generosity in allowing us to describe aspects of their work.

Julie Diamond's editorial comments were especially helpful in challenging us to create more. Kate Jobe, Dawn Menken, and Leslie Heizer helped with finishing touches. Jan Loeken, George Mecouch, Jim Beggs, Reini Hauser, Nisha Zenoff, Diane Ozan, Max Schupbach, and Gary Reiss saved us from the worst errors. Michael Toms from New Dimensions Radio helped us to edit out superfluous dialogue.

The last chapters were a special project for us. Arny and I re-created Chapter 13 after having been awakened by Carl and Pearl Mindell to what they saw as the compelling similarity between

Buddhist thought and process work. We are indebted to both of them. Robin Waterfield, our editor from Penguin Arkana in London, also helped shape these chapters with one of his comments:

> It is one of the bees in my bonnet that twentieth-century psychological terms are, in a spiritual context, a misleading veneer over the older, more traditional religious terminology. All too often, in the twentieth century, people feel ashamed to admit to the fact that they have religious feelings and want to express them. Psychology and psychological language can feed this fear, whereas it ought to be freeing people from it, and allowing them to express their religiousness fully or more fully.

This workshop occurred before I took a more active role as a co-leader in seminars with Arny. However, my interest in the philosophical and spiritual foundations of process work was there from the beginning of our relationship and inspired me to transcribe and help birth the following for you.

Amy Mindell
Oregon, 1990

PART I

Theory and Practice

CHAPTER 1

Riding the Horse Backwards

We arrived at Esalen on Friday evening. It was dark and misty, and we could hear the eerie sound of the ocean in the distance. As we showered and got ready for dinner, people knocked on our door and asked if they could break the rules and get into the seminar at the last moment!

We wondered what was awaiting us and what the people would be like. I was scared as usual, but Arny was relaxed—he almost fell asleep before the seminar. On our way to the dining hall we saw a large group of people registering for our seminar. While we were eating many people came up to us and greeted us with, "Hello, so you are Amy and Arny."

After dinner we went to Huxley, Esalen's largest conference room, where our seminar was to be held. This spacious and wood-panelled room overlooking the Pacific was filled with many soft cushions for sitting. Arny sat quietly in front of the blackboard. The participants came in and sat in a circle around the room. Arny waited in silence for a few minutes before starting. I stepped outside the circle and began videotaping the proceedings. I felt a sort of relaxation in the air in spite of the tension of being in the midst of a new group. Arny looked around at the group and began to speak.

ARNY: I'd like to meet each of you because I don't know you yet.
One fun way of finding out who you are, instead of just going
around and saying your names, is to create "spots" in the
room. Let's imagine this space to be a field. [*Arny gets up and
walks to the center of the circle.*] Let's see, what are the different
reasons you have for coming here? One of them must be to
work on yourselves.

Many people nod their heads.

This spot here, on the right hand side of the circle, is for those
members of the group who came here to work on themselves.

Another reason for coming must be for professional training reasons. [*He walks to the far left of the circle.*] This spot on the
left hand side of the circle is for people who came for training.
Are there any other spots or reasons for coming I've left out?

One of the participants says jokingly that he has come for a vacation by the sea. Everyone bursts out laughing. Arny then continues.

Right. That important spot will go over there behind the
other two. Are there any others? OK.

Now, decide on one of the reasons that you are here. It
must not be the *only* reason, just the first one. I'd like to meet
you if you'd like to introduce yourself by standing in one of
these spots. If you feel that it's not right for you to get up and
do something so extroverted, you don't have to. You can stay
on the periphery of the circle. There is no rule that says you
must express yourselves. No expression also tells me how to
respect where you are.

Vacation by the sea

✗

Professional training ✗   ✗ Personal work

Group field in the beginning

Many participants rise spontaneously, one after another and shyly, happily, aggressively, or fearfully go to the designated spots and introduce themselves. Some live here at Esalen, others have come for professional training, still others have come for play or for fun. Many have come to iron out inner problems. The initial shyness recedes as people get to know one another and get to know the group's field of interest in this way. Everyone sits again. Arny glances around the room at the participants and begins to speak in a quiet and intense manner.

> This weekend I'd like to give you a taste of various aspects of what is rapidly developing into a process-oriented psychology. There are many aspects to process work and many different kinds of seminars. Some seminars are based upon themes like chronic symptoms or childhood dreams, others focus on relationship or movement, inner work, death, and dying or the living Tao. But this weekend we shall concentrate on introducing and pulling these various areas together.
>
> Process work is something like a pie where each section has its own flavor.

Arny draws a diagram of the process-work pie on the board and discusses how each of the sections are different aspects of process work.

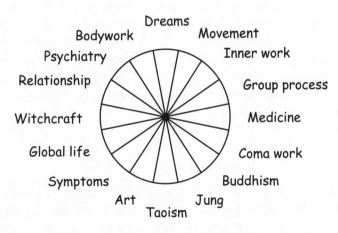

The process-work pie

In this workshop I'd like to give you a taste of some of the main pie sections and a slice of what I consider at the moment to be the essence of process—Taoism. This evening I will talk with you about theory and do some experiential exercises [*See Chapters 1, 2 and 3*]. Tomorrow morning I'd like to experiment with working internally and to focus on problems people have working on themselves alone [*See Chapters 4 and 5*]. Tomorrow morning I'd also like to show, with Amy's help, process-oriented movement work, which is a rapid way of accessing dreams and the dreaming process [*See Chapter 5*].

Tomorrow afternoon we will do bodywork and focus on chronic symptoms, learning to work with our hands, to switch channels and to read the dreaming background from hands-on work [*See Chapters 6 and 7*]. Saturday evening it might be exciting to do an open seat to work on whatever is in the air or, rather, fish up and swim with whatever is in the sea [*See Chapters 8 and 9*].

And then, Sunday morning, my choice is to show you some rapid ways of working on relationship and group issues without much pain [*See Chapters 10 and 11*]. So, if our group process permits, you'll see some different aspects of process work in the ten hours which are allotted to us.

There are many aspects of process work which we will not cover here, for example, working with people in comas and working with old people and small children. A fascinating aspect of process work that we can do together another time is working with extreme and altered states, especially with people with psychotic breaks. It's important and exciting work. We are now in the midst of beginning a psychosomatic and extreme states clinic in the Process Work Center of Portland, Oregon.

Autobiographical Chatter

Since you have introduced yourselves, perhaps I should tell you about who I am, how I got here today and my state of knowledge about the philosophy which structures process work.

Arny pauses and looks down for a moment. He looks up and speaks, though remaining very quiet.

> In this very moment I am in a very quiet spot. I'm surprised. This quietness has been going on for a few months with me. It's like I am sitting by the sea. Something huge is breathing in my ear. Just telling you about it makes me feel very close to the sea. There are so many things I am involved in outwardly that I am surprised at this inner quiet.
>
> If you see me sometimes looking very quiet and introverted, it doesn't mean you can't come over and talk. Just join me even if I look like I'm meditating. Use me. I'm here this weekend for you. If you catch me at the dinner table, please come over. I'm here for it. I don't get abused easily, so just feel free and do it!

Many people around the room smile when he says this.

> You know, process work began years ago for me, as I was finishing my Jungian training, which I loved. I knew a lot about dreams, but was unable to work with myself on a physical level. I had aches and pains and physical symptoms, which I didn't know how to work with. So I developed a method that was originally based on the concept of Jungian psychology which values what happens to us. Out of these experiences came my first book, *Dreambody*.
>
> I could never completely buy the idea of pathology. After studying Jungian psychology you have the idea, or rather the experience, that events are meaningful. The idea that I should think of myself as being sick if I had a pain in my leg didn't feel right. I did not trust the voice in my mind which said, "Arny, you are ill if your body is off." That is the voice of our normal world.
>
> I had another, more loving voice, which said, "Maybe what's happening to you is like a dream!" So I took a guess. Since I've always considered my dreams meaningful, I thought that maybe what was happening in my body was meaningful too, not just pathological or wrong. That's how I developed process-oriented psychology. From this idea and experiment

came my discovery of the dreambody, which you can read about in *Working with the Dreaming Body*.

But, you know, this is only part of the story. The other half of the story is that I was not enjoying myself enough in my practice. Since I had no money, I needed to work as much as possible. Psychology was my livelihood. And since I had to work a lot, I became restless with my practice. First of all, it was too serious. There was too little creativity and art in it, too much talk and too little movement. I liked the intellectual challenge of my work, but I could not stand sitting in my chair so much. After all, I loved running, bicycling and skiing. I don't really know what was wrong; perhaps I just needed to move more. Moreover, I couldn't find a place for my interest in global problems in my private practice.

I got frustrated talking about the unconscious. Like others, I wanted to live it and experiment with it more directly. I'm afraid that I became a great problem for myself and for my teachers. I am still a bit of a problem for myself! One part of me is very conservative, serious, loves studying and learning, and has trouble with the side which just wants to live. While one part of me bows in awe before the numinous, the other wants to play with it. I imagine we are all like that, at least some of the time.

After discovering the dreambody concept, I ran into a personal crisis. I was talking with a friend in Zurich, who was taking his exams in philosophy. We were having an exciting and fun discussion when suddenly he popped up with something that utterly shocked me and for which I'm very thankful.

It sounds strange to have a personal crisis around a philosophical issue, but I want to share this with you now. My friend made me realize that the way I had been thinking and the way I had been practicing was based upon the Cartesian coordinate system, upon Newtonian physics and upon the idea that matter and psyche are different and can be separated! It's taken me seventeen years to find my way out of that crisis and it's only last month that I found the roots of it.

You see, working with the body led me straight into this crisis because I could no longer describe what happened in my practice in terms of the language of bodywork or of dream work. I thought to myself, "What am I doing? I'm not working just with the body, nor just with dreams." I wondered if it was a form of energy work, but the word "energy" had lost its excitement for me since my studies in physics. I knew that energy had no significance unto itself, but was a vague, and therefore weak, description of the Tao. Then I began to wonder why I had to describe my work with terms such as "psychic" or "somatic," "matter" or "spirit."

The need for different languages in psychology, biochemistry, physics and mysticism disturbed me intensely. I finally had to drop the whole problem and develop a more neutral and practical language. The vocabulary systems that I had been using from Jungian psychology and from bodywork were no longer useful in working with people going through strongly altered states. Jung obviously knew about this problem because in his last writings, his *Mysterium Coniunctionis*, he posits a neutral language, which will eventually join physics and psychology.

Strangely enough, it was my background in physics which returned to help me in this crisis over Cartesian thinking. One section of physics, the so-called "phenomenological theory of irreversible, coupled processes," gave me the idea to formulate human events independently of how they occurred. I liked this section of physics because it reminded me of the ancient Mystery schools. It approaches events phenomenologically; processes occur, connect and are coupled, even though we cannot yet explain how or why.

That was for me: working with what is happening instead of trying to explain its origins! Maybe the idea of origins is only one part of reality. Perhaps there is a complementary view which says that nothing originates; it just exists.

Then a differentiated concept of process occurred to me which was more specific and exact. I realized that process is the change in what we observe, the flow of signals and the messages they carry! Simple. This definition was more differentiated than "energy" and more exact than the vague, New Age concepts of process. It was more neutral than the language of dream analysis or bodywork. The new language describes the information structure of process, something we'll talk about shortly.

I realized that I had been living through a crisis as if I had been in the seventeenth century. This surprised me. I thought at first that my problems were just personal, that I was just suffering from growing pains like a typical teenager, outgrowing teachers and parents, and trying to find new ways of thinking. But it was much more complicated than that! I was stuck in history, like most of us are, trying to decide on whether something was inner or outer, psyche or matter, due to neural disturbances or due to the collective unconscious. I was trying to find the origins, causes, and locations of events instead of working with the process which was happening.

Thus when I began thinking about the dreambody in the early 1970s I never dreamed that I would get into something like process work! I can tell you, I personally would never have had the courage to plan it. The topic seems too vast for me, and as far as my outer life goes, well, there are too many people and telephone calls!

The group laughs. Arny's way of talking personally creates a warm and cozy atmosphere.

The Process Paradigm

So you see, dreambodywork led to the concept of process and channels. And this, in turn, opened me up to relationships, meditation, psychiatry, work with the dying, global issues and conflict resolution. All of these areas are just different applications of the same paradigm.

I think, for therapists to be awake and successful, we need to be able to know something of all the areas of psychology. To do global work, for example, we need to be able to do relationship work and inner work, because peace cannot be maintained if an individual needs inner help. But inner work is not enough, either. We need to understand group processing because, even if everyone is quietly centered in themselves, the group still has to learn to live and work together. A group which is not together will throw each individual out of kilter.

But even knowing all of these skills is not enough if we are not connected to a certain transpersonal something, which has to do with belief in what others might call the apparently absurd or impossible. You shall soon see that I look for the absurd, the nonsensical thing in an individual or group, the thing which others ignore. I look for the spirit of the incomprehensible statement, gesture or error and then care for it and let it unfold. I will soon share with you technical details about how this incomprehensible signal appears and how to work with it, but just let me stress here, at the outset, that the gold lies in the messages which we do not intend to send.

Caring for the absurd and impossible is like believing the world is round when everyone else thinks the world is flat. Following the unwanted, unintended message goes against collective belief, which says that if you follow the unknown, it will lead you off the edge of the world. We all think that when we get to the edge of the known world, we will surely fall off. But process work shows the roundness of our universe. It shows that if we have the courage to follow unintentional signals to their edges, we do not fall off, but discover new worlds.

Indeed, those of you who have ventured a bit into the impossible know that the world is really round, and that this roundness is a momentous discovery. Life is so round! Even near death you sense yourself going on. At the edge, things transform and new worlds open up.

Thus the process-oriented approach is interesting because you must reverse your normal mode of consciousness, or, to use a metaphor, you need to ride a horse backwards. One of the Native American tribes had a funny trickster figure who was a little strange. He was allowed to stay in the tribe as long as he could be called "the reversed one," the one who did everything differently. His horse went forwards but he rode it sitting in a reversed position, facing backwards.

Riding the horse backwards means saying to life, "Yes, it's impossible," but also, "How interesting this disease might be." You go forwards in a backwards way. Normally you think death is awful, but in a reversed and heretical way you could also think that death might teach you something. It could even be exciting! You say "no" to pain, and then, when nothing else works, try saying "yes" to pain. You'll jump for joy and grin when trouble turns into something interesting. It's mercurial and fun. It's like a religious experience or the ability to be negative. In the process work paradigm there is a complex "yes" to the world as a potential, as a seed for something trying to unfold.

I have a complex relationship to thinking and understanding. Earlier I needed to think before acting. Now I trust nature and do less thinking. Instead I follow my feelings. It is my present way to follow the unpredictable. I act now and think later. Therefore I often work ahead of my thinking and become one-sided. There is much I do not understand about how process work operates. Some things I can explain, but there's a lot I want to study. The business of facilitating human processes is a wide-open subject, as ancient as Taoism but as new as the holomovement theories of the universe. And I want to ask your help and give you the feeling that we are all incredibly responsible for the development of psychology.

Process Work and Other Psychological Practices

There are moments when process work looks like another therapy or meditation procedure. You will see role play and think, "Oh, that's Gestalt." When we work with myths and fairy tales, it looks Jungian. The attention to awareness seems like Vipassanna meditation, and the belief in events is Taoism. Some of you may see connections to Haikomi, massage, bioenergetics or other forms of bodywork.

Looking back, it seems as if I developed process-oriented psychology in a monastery. I needed a lot of inner work, and

Switzerland shielded me from the world. It is only since I have been at Esalen that I have seen others work, thanks in great part to the in-house video library.

Since my training was in Jungian psychology, I thought process work was an extension of Jungian work. Now some of the Gestalt teachers here have shown me that process work is an advance in Gestalt practice. In process work the facilitator is not only a reflector, but a whole living person. Process theory says that there is no inside or outside to an individual's process; there is only awareness of how it changes and flows.

Thus, as well as that which goes on "inside" of you, even the environment is part of your process. Everyone agrees that you and I are separate, but we also know from personal experiences, from relationships and from modern physics that there are no definite boundaries between you and me. We cannot say exactly where you end and I begin.

The discovery that what happens to you is part of me translates for the facilitator into the practice of being a whole person, being inside and outside the client's process at the same time. There are some moments when we can no longer even know whose process it is! Thus, movement, contact, and relationship are as important as inner feelings and dreams, and we place as much emphasis on awareness as on behavior. We shall come back to this point later in the seminar. The basic idea of process work is to develop therapy and facilitation procedures based on the entire situation we are in; thus, for brief periods, process work must look like known meditation or therapeutic practices. Perhaps the very namelessness or adaptability of process work is, paradoxically, its most specific nature. It has a hard scientific core of awareness and information theory, and yet, though it produces mundane, practical results, has a mystical element in it, depending upon the practitioner.

In a way, process-oriented psychology has only awareness as a technique; it uses whatever the process demands in the moment: Buddhism, Jungian psychology, NLP (neurolinguistic programming), Gestalt, Rolfing, Haikomi or anything else we have not yet dreamed of. Psychological methods are patterns inherent in all of us at given times. Therefore process work is more of an attitude towards people and towards nature than it is a set of techniques.

I like process work because of the compassion it has, because of how it values your momentary, living unconscious, because of its relationship to its very old ancestor, Taoism. According to the ancients, the Tao, or the Way, was also nameless and had a thousand names. Isn't that a great definition of the Tao? What difference does it make what you call it?

Who can follow the Tao, or nature? It is very difficult. It's easy to observe and follow the things you like, but following nature means also noticing, remembering, and following the things you don't like. That is a subtle project! I don't mind noticing what I want to do and what I like, but, wow, it's tough picking up on the things which are absurd or unintentional, and that is where the most important things are!

Once I have become aware of things I normally don't notice, I come to a second problem, which the Taoists did not talk much about: that is, how to unfold, or "cook," awareness and events so that they reveal their essence. The flow of events, of nature or the Tao, becomes meaningful only when we interact with, amplify, and unfold its contents. Otherwise it is only a mystery waiting to be discovered.

Process work has a broad spectrum of application. It works with little kids and old-timers. It works with clients in most states: they can be awake or asleep, alone or with others. After doing lots of coma work, Amy and I often joke with each other and say, "As long as someone is breathing, they'll surely want to work on themselves or even dance!" One goal of mine, which I may never reach, is to be able to work with any human being or any group in any state. I am not quite there yet, but it is a goal worth striving for.

Process work needs many different types of therapists because of the many different kinds of states people get into. It needs therapists who are already practicing their own specific work, and who are interested in adding the process orientation to their medicine bag of possibilities. All of the different

schools of psychology and related disciplines, the Gestalt therapists, behaviorists, Rolfers, transpersonal psychologists, spiritual healers, shamans, and all of the others obviously need to
be developing their own approaches and creating a part of the
pie.

Yet, even as it is important for all of them to do their own
things as best they can, there is also a growing need to get
together, to unify therapy, spiritual practice, ecology, and art.
The different schools stay away from one another not only to
develop their individual approaches, but also because they do
not yet have a unifying paradigm which they all agree upon!
Some believe it all began in childhood; others, before the individual was born; still others think only of the here and now.
Shamans work mediumistically, Western psychologists behave
as if they were trained, Eastern schools recommend forgetting
yourself.

Even then, most of us do not do what we say we are
doing! Some therapists say there are no "shoulds," and then
command their clients to do things, instead of offering an
intervention as a possibility. Others say they follow the individual while giving behavioral prescriptions. Some say they are
rational while irrationally raising the mind to the position of
divinity.

Under these circumstances, where we are all doing our
own things, the only thing that unifies us is the fact that each
of us is trying to follow her own personality, her own process!
Therefore anything, like process work, that studies human
processes automatically attempts to unify therapy and art, shamanism, and spiritual practice.

My spiritual belief is that reality is potentially divine.
Everything that is, lies enfolded in our total perceptual system.
Psychological beliefs, theories, and paradigms are special feeling attitudes, particular states of mind which come to us when
we are confronted by specific states and problems. I have often
observed how something like the process work paradigm
always appears in us when causal approaches don't work or

when life becomes too complex to be rationally comprehensible. Most human situations are just too weird to make sense.

The present global situation, our ecological and relationship problems are at that confusing and incomprehensible point right now! Process ideas state that, in principle, a causal approach to problems can be part of the process. For example, you can get sick by eating the wrong food. Causality is important. It is usually the way your mind works in the beginning of a process. The causal approach fights what happens. It doesn't let it happen. But then, when you have gone through and lost that causal fight, you still have one last option left: to get along with the thing which is bothering you.

STEVE: I like what you are saying. It sounds important, but I suspect that I could never follow it.

ARNY: I understand. Then you must not try. To tell you the truth I myself don't follow what I preach all the time. I can't. I don't want to follow everything! Resistance to processes is also a process. Unconsciousness or lack of awareness is also part of nature. You cannot "not follow." You can only choose to be aware or not be aware of what is happening. We all follow our process, even when we don't!

Perceptions and Awareness

Our job is to become aware of how we and others perceive things. When we help these perceptions to unfold, creating fluid processes where static states previously reigned, unexpected discoveries and enrichment follow. Notice how people identify themselves, and try to appreciate that; and also notice how ready they are to change these identities with new discoveries. I try to wait for the moment in which I can unravel or unfold some combination of the possible and impossible.

In *Working with the Dreaming Body* and *River's Way* I speak about many theories. But regardless of the scientific formulation, the process worker must develop a sense for that part of nature which is neglected and which needs greater respect. It is like riding the horse backwards.

Examples

Consider, for example, a man whose chronic symptom is coldness. He not only needs warmth but also more coldness, since the persistence of this state implies that it has a message which needs to unfold.

How do we unfold the experience behind his freezing? Notice how he perceives it. Note who is upset by this freezing, and appreciate what it means in the moment for him that he is sick. Then nourish the impossible.

When he says that he is cold, I notice that he trembles slightly. I appreciate that he thinks he is ill, but then I support these shakes. When I support or amplify these tremors, he enters into an unexpected vibratory or even ecstatic experience. He shakes, and with encouragement, also drums and begins to dance. His coldness turns into an expression of his maleness, which he has not even dreamed about.

Or, for example, a woman who wanted to know the meaning of life sat down to work with me and tossed her handbag on the floor. But the way she tossed her bag had something weird about it. In fact, I suspected that it contained the somatic answer to her question about the meaning of life. Here was not just a toss. The way she tossed that bag, when encouraged to happen consciously, became a hand flip and then turned into a dance of life, of just letting things happen, throwing it all away and enjoying herself. She became ecstatic when her dance answered her question about the meaning of life.

What really made her so excited and happy? I suspect that it was the experience of wholeness. Being whole, having access to all of our known and unknown parts, is consciousness. This type of access and awareness is an ecstatic experience. What else is there? It is wonderful to live fully, to live your totality, at least for a few moments.

All right, now it's time to work. The theory feels finished for the moment. Let's get down to practice and experience things.

CHAPTER 2

Dream and Body Processes

T he first evening continues as Arny illustrates the theory of process-oriented psychology with some experiential exercises.

ARNY: I don't think it is wise for anyone to identify as a student or to be a passive listener for more than fifteen minutes at a time. That is why I want to give you a chance to experiment with ideas on your own. Instead of talking about the division between matter and psyche, let's work with your physical experiences or symptoms that have caught your attention recently. Is there anyone here who has a pain, symptom or body problem that they are aware of?

There is silence. No one raises a hand. The group breaks into laughter.

Your laughter is very important! After all, who wants to focus on a problem? But remember, having body problems is like having dreams. It's a healthy thing to dream, just as it is to have your body producing symptoms. From the process work point of view, it's important that your body creates symptoms. It means you are alive and dreaming.

Being ill is also terrible. We know what it is like to be a victim. But it is not necessarily a sign that you are bad, sick or unconscious, or that you have sinned against God. It is first and foremost a sign that you have a powerful dreaming process happening. In fact, the stronger the symptom, the more powerful the individuation process at a given moment, so *congratulations for being ill!*

Now, try to feel or remember one of the body problems that you have or have had. Choose one which you can feel, or have felt in the past. Bring that feeling up to your awareness now.

Arny pauses for a moment to let the participants feel a symptom. After a moment of silence, Larry, a man in the group, asks, "Suppose someone has a body feeling that he is not feeling?"

ARNY [*Turns to him*]: Do you have one right now?

LARRY: No, but I wonder how it is possible to feel something that you're not feeling?

ARNY: Not feeling something usually means feeling a whole lot of "something" which you're not wanting to feel. It's very important. If somebody says she is not feeling something, I say, "Go ahead and don't feel the something that you're feeling." That is, tell me what it is you're filtering out of awareness.

Of course it is also possible that the symptom is experienced in a channel other than feeling, but "not feeling" is usually still feeling. Feel one of these body problems you feel or do not feel, and amplify it by feeling it more exactly.

LARRY [*To Arny excitedly*]: Thanks! I get it. I just felt an old pain in my knee that I used to have.

ARNY: Super. [*Turns to the rest of the group*] Go ahead and feel that knee, or any other symptom. Now I want you to feel that as exactly as you can. Just feeling it is important. Feel it and increase or amplify that feeling. Feel the pressure, temperature, the location of the pain. Extend where you feel it and experiment with feeling a small feeling throughout your whole body.

The room becomes silent as many people close their eyes and work internally on their symptoms. Arny continues to speak slowly and quietly.

> Try feeling it more. When you're ready, try to make a picture of the feeling that you're having. Not any general picture, but a picture that represents the particular feeling that you're having in your symptom or body right now. Take your time. Make a picture of the feeling that you're having and then, if you can, allow that picture to unfold as if you were going to the movies. Let the picture go on. Don't just stay with the frozen feeling or picture, but let it unfold.

Arny pauses and allows people to feel, amplify and see their feelings.

> Now ask yourself the following question. Have you recently dreamed, in the last days or months or years, something like the picture that you are seeing now? Have you ever seen such a picture before, or one that is somehow associated with it? Or have you dreamed about figures who do the same thing as the ones in your present picture?
>
> Were you able to do this? Could you go to the movies? Were you able to connect it with a dream or dreamlike experience in everyday life?

Many people nod their heads and say yes.

HENRY: Yes, I felt my eczema. It felt raw and terrible. I amplified the feeling and the picture which came out finally surprised me. Ugh! I saw a bird, and it dug its way through my flesh and then flew into the sky. Then I let this unfold as you said and as I saw it flying I remembered a dream in which I befriended a bird!

ARNY: Well, that is the dreambody. Instead of talking about it, I wanted you to experience it first. Some of you might have had trouble feeling and making pictures. I'll help you with it during this weekend.

"Dreambody" is the name for the experience which expresses itself through your body sensations and in your dreams as well. The dreambody is first a sensation and, then, finally a message which appears in your body, in your dreams and in many other channels too. Your unconscious utilizes various sensory channels, each of which gives the same message. Whether visual images or physical experiences, the messages are the same. That invariance, or symmetry, as scientists say, is what I call the "dreambody."

Channels

Now you can understand how difficult it is to say whether the dreambody is dreamlike or physical. So let's use the more neutral information language, which is neither dream nor body specific. When I speak in terms of seeing, or visual experiences and feeling, or proprioceptive experiences, I am using a neutral language, a signal and information language which is neither mind nor body.

Now, I want to ask you to make a movement that goes along with that particular body feeling you were having when working on the body symptom. In process work we call the experience of movement kinesthesis. Go ahead and make a movement which expresses the feeling and visualization which you had when working on your symptom.

People begin to move and some make small gestures. Others stand up, swing and jump. Arny notices all the movements beginning to happen and says, "Now, did you notice the particular movement you made? Go ahead and let it move more and complete itself. Try it." The movements become more comprehensible as the bending, jumping, shaking and breathing unfold.

Have you noticed or do you remember that movement in the past? Hasn't it been trying to appear before? You probably make it spontaneously a lot, which means it has been a movement asking for integration, just like a dream or body problem. This movement represents not only inner feelings you may have been looking for, but may also put together many dreams as well. Lots of your movements, especially incomplete movements, are bits and pieces of these dreams.

HENRY: I went on with the bird just now with movement, and it turned into a sort of cuddling motion, but with God. Gee, it's unbelievable!

ARNY: That's very touching. [*He pauses a moment.*] Now we can also work backwards. We can start with dreams. Let's take for example, a recent dream in which I saw a carpenter hammering something on the side of his house. I'm in the middle of building a house in the mountains so I had this dream. What body experience would go along with that particular image?

STEVE: A pulsing feeling.

ARNY: Yes. I used to have the feeling of a strong heartbeat that did not seem to quiet down. And what incomplete body motion might that dream and feeling go along with?

A participant makes a repetitive punching motion with her arm. Arny watches her and agrees, "Yes, spasms like this." He clenches his fist and begins to make a hammering gesture with his right forearm. He stops the motion midway and rests his arm on his knee before the motion is completed.

And in walking? How would this movement look in my walk? [*He gets up and begins to walk around the inside of the circle and steps down just a bit harder with the heel of his left foot.*] Dreaming is very subtle. Can you see me hammering with my left foot? [*He walks back to his seat and sits.*]

These spontaneous signals in all our channels are expressions of the same message. And in relationships? Can you

The carpenter dream image in movement

imagine how that hammering could manifest itself while I was talking to somebody? Let's say Amy and I are having some sort of relationship thing and I say, "Amy, you know, I think you're terrific and..." [*As he talks he simultaneously drums with his fingers on his knee.*] What am I doing?

People point to his finger motions.

That's right. What I'd really like to do is [*Smacking his leg*] really hammer, and say to her, "YOU ARE AMAZING!"

Everyone laughs.

So, there are different channels with the same information in the background. The hammerer is trying to come out.

Healing

You know, healing and health are very Cartesian considerations. What happens if you work with me and my fast heartbeat, and I start pounding on the ground to demonstrate the feeling? If you help me complete this process, I might realize that I want to build not only a house, but a new world. If I pick up that information and really begin doing it, then my heartbeat changes. A healer would notice that my heartbeat has changed and say I'm healed. In his mind, I'm changed for the better. Healing is one way of talking about the change, but it's a Cartesian consideration. What really happened to me? Why did my heart rate go down?

MARTHA: You externalized it.

ARNY: I externalized it. I integrated a piece of myself. That is analytical thinking, good. Is there another way of looking at it?

DON: You processed the information.

ARNY: Yes, I processed the information. I got the message and it changed. The message sender, in this case a heart, no longer sent the message which it had in mind for me. Behaving differently made me feel differently. I had different images of life and my movement relaxed.

The difference in feeling corresponds to cure or healing. If you get a message, you feel differently and for some reason, your physical chemistry changes as well. Feeling is crucial: it is a direct perception of body condition; it is fluid and process-oriented, and plays a central role in our work.

In any case, in medical thinking, a healing took place. In analytical terms this healing would be due to the integration of a dream figure. In witchcraft the healing might be explained as having occurred through overcoming some evil being, satisfying a frustrated spirit, or overcoming someone who had been holding me back.

The phenomenological and sensory-grounded fact is that a change in feeling occurred because a part of me which is too easygoing got the hammering message. Then a mystery occurred which I cannot explain. When I get a message, my physical chemistry and anatomy change without my knowing the details of how this occurs. It simply does.

If we work with signals and messages, we work phenomenologically and do not focus upon physical chemistry. Yet changes occur there. It is like a Mystery School teaching. Know and perceive and work with it and the world changes. Or is this art? Is the incomplete movement involved with dream images the beginning of a dance and creativity? I think it is. Then this is art, not only physics, chemistry, psychology or healing. In the moment the concept of art fits what I do more than the other descriptions.

Healing is really a very limited idea. It deals only with cause and effect. It has little art to it. It does not focus on my ability to dance and move, my ability to visualize, or the creativity of the force behind the symptom.

We all fear our symptoms and want to heal them. We go to all kinds of healers, not realizing that our worst problem is not the sickness, but that we are hypnotized by culture into believing that what we experience is bad and has to be repressed and healed instead of lived and loved.

On Channels and Professions

One of the reasons for talking about channels is that the way we work as therapists is usually very channel-oriented. If you're not conscious of the kinds of channels that you're using, you'll find yourself using the same two or three channels all the time. If you're a body therapist you'll use touch, that is movement and proprioception, but may inhibit visualizations. As a dream analyst you might work visually with people and forget movement. As a family therapist you might do relationship work but not dreams or movement. Similarly, the average politician thinks only of masses of people and too little about individuals.

Most people get bored after a few years if they practice the same thing every day. They know or can calculate ahead of time what they will be doing with people. They feel secure at the expense of their creativity, and therefore get burned out, not because they are tired, but because they are depressed by their professions.

That's why thinking in terms of channels can be very important. No one has to love working with people all the time, but the reason you start to hate it is almost always that you are using only a limited number of channels. It's not just the people. You're not just burnt out by helping. You need more feeling or movement, more inner work, more family work or more of a global context.

The channels I will be focusing on in this seminar are seeing, feeling or proprioception, hearing, moving or kinesthesia, and relating or experiencing our senses in another person. We shall just touch on the world as a channel, and probably will not have time to work on the spiritual channel or parapsychological experiences.

Body Experience

Proprioception

Seeing   Movement

Mind   **World**

Hearing   Relating

World

Process Channel Pie

Dreams, Programming and Processing

I want to do an exercise to show you the difference between programming and processing. But first let me say something that you will not believe: *Having a process is still a new idea.*

Everyone speaks of living the unconscious, of the Self, of God, of inner wisdom, of following yourself and all that stuff. But when it comes down to it, we just don't trust ourselves or our perceptions enough, and do not really follow our own processes. We do not value what we see, hear, feel, how we move, relate or experience the world. No wonder so many people always feel criticized or unloved! They hate their own perceptions, and thus do not follow themselves. They cannot follow their own individual processes, but instead program themselves until they can't stand it any more.

Having and following your own individual process is therefore the oldest but the newest idea. Perhaps it will never be fashionable, or at least not yet! Yet it is what most of us want in our heart of hearts.

Would you like to try another experiment? Try turning to whoever is sitting next to you and ask them what they are dreaming or have been dreaming about. Then see if you can develop your dreamwork from what they say. How can you do that? The most fun way is to develop your dreamwork from your client's conscious concerns and unconscious behavior. It's useful to consider that the best interventions are always those which are already trying to happen. Let me explain.

Most of you already know various forms of dreamwork and have developed dreamwork tools, but now let's drop our programs and develop our awareness. Let me be your first client. I will tell you a dream of my own first and ask all of you to work with me on it. After the demonstration, let's try this with the dreamer next to you.

What are you aware of when I tell my dream? You are all my therapists. [*Pauses, then begins to tell his dream*] This afternoon, before the seminar, I had a dream about a man [*Adjusts his glasses as he talks*] who called himself Fire. Now Fire and I wrestled and after a while we formed a square. [*He outlines a square in the air with his hands.*] Fire and I wrestled and somehow out of what happened between us we created a square. And in the center of the square was a blue iridescent point. [*He makes a point in the air with his hands.*] That is the end of the dream.

Now, how will you work with me and why? This is harder than telling you to interpret my dream or doing Gestalt or any other technique.

A participant, Bill, asks Arny what his associations to fire are. Rather than answering, Arny asks him why he asked that question.

BILL: Well, it's something you are wrestling with in the dream that is significant to you.

ARNY: Great. I was hoping you'd pick up the emphasis on fire. I not only said I dreamed about it, but I used the word "fire" several times when I was telling my dream. And hearing me saying it several times, you realized I was unconsciously trying to stress the word fire. Therefore the best intervention with my dream at that point would be to ask for a word association, because the word association stresses special words.

BILL: I would see that as the central point. It is as if you are the central point now, in anticipation of what you're going to go through. You're giving off a lot of energy, which is fire, and the struggle means being as clear and accurate as you want to be with that energy. The point in that wrestling match is a focal point of what you are doing right now.

As Bill is interpreting the dream, Arny watches him and looks down frequently. He's also wiggling his toes.

ARNY: Good. Now while you were talking to me, what sorts of feedback were you getting from me as the dreamer?

BILL: Basically that you were looking at it and it was pretty accurate.

ARNY: Did anyone else notice my feedback? Looking for feedback is an important aspect of process work because the dreamer's feedback tells us whether you are on the right or wrong track with your interventions. To save your energy and enjoy yourself the most, be very careful about the feedback

that you get from the dreamer before employing an intervention. The right intervention can be wrong if given in the
wrong moment.

You picked up only one signal of my feedback, the positive one. You saw me looking at you, acting like a good client,
and appreciating your attempt to understand me, but at the
same time my toes were busy and I frequently looked down. I
was behaving like a typically good client, supporting my therapist and trapping him.

I enjoyed your attempt to help me, but some of your interpretation did not fit. I love interpretation, but not before I get
a chance to experience the dream. My sermon is, "Check out
the feedback."

Let's think for a moment. What are the many possible reasons people tell dreams? Only one little one is to get an interpretation. Another might be to avoid feeling. And still another
could be to gain greater access to life in that moment.

BILL: Thanks, I like that. I know I like interpreting. I can't stop
sometimes.

ARNY: Sure, you enjoy interpreting. OK. It's good that you know
that. But be careful. Check out the feedback to your intervention to see if it is the right one for the client. Only the
dreamer can determine whether something is right or wrong.
The size of your clientele depends upon your ability to pick
up and change with feedback. There is no right or wrong in
process work. There is only on or off the process! What else
did the rest of you notice?

CHERYL: I'd ask you if you feel the struggle in any particular place
in your body right now.

ARNY: That connects to channels that I'm using, my internal
proprioception. You're helping me connect my dreams with
my body. [*To everyone*] Did you watch me when I told the
dream? I'm going to tell the dream again rapidly and you
watch and see different things that I'm doing this time.

I had a dream where I was wrestling with a man named Fire
and I underline the word fire. And then something happened

and we formed a square. [*He outlines the square with his hands.*] Finally a point appeared in the center of that square.

How did I tell you the dream this time?

SHELLY: With movement.

ARNY: I was using movement. So here at this particular point in the dream, where I outline the square with my hands, it would be helpful to use movement. You might ask me, for example, to make that movement again, to do it more consciously and go on with it. When I was talking, the movements I was making were hardly conscious. I almost did not know how I did them. [*Arny goes back to the dream.*] And then somehow there was this beautiful iridescent thing right in the center of the square. [*He points in the air with his hand.*]

JOAN: You used your hands.

ARNY: Yes, I used my hands and what sort of language did I use? What did I say?

DAN: You said "beautiful!"

ARNY: Yes, I stressed the word "beautiful." Is this not a visual word? So how would you work visually with that part of the dream?

MELISSA: You could add color to it.

ARNY: Yes, that would be helpful. And have me see it colorfully and paint it in my head. Could I make that color more intense? And if you work carefully with me and watch my cues and feedback, the dream will interpret itself.

This self-explanation is an experiment and a discovery that you can make. The hypothesis is that if you pick up on the processes which are happening, the dream will be self-explanatory, self-revealing. Jung said it another way. He said dreams are their own analysis or interpretation.

Take a few minutes. Don't go into the entire dreamwork but experiment with the person next to you. Put your methods of dreamwork aside and ask, look and listen. Is the person telling the dream underlining words like fire? Then do that with her. Ask her for a word association. That is her way of working with that part of the dream.

Is he using lots of intense visual imagery? Then work visually. If he is using movement, then work with completing his
movement. If she has relationship trouble with you, then you
would have to address that.

What would you do if he was talking to somebody else in
the dream? What if I started telling a dream like this: "I was
talking to this guy, and I said 'You son of a bitch. You nasty
guy.' And then he said…" What sort of dreamwork would be
really great here?

JOHN: Dialogue.

ARNY: Dialogue! That's where psychodrama or Gestalt is ideal.
Doing anything else with that part of the dream would be fine,
but probably less useful. The dreamer has her own way of
working on dreams. Let the person next to you tell a dream
and see if you can pick up the methods that you would use if
you were to follow his or her process.

MARIA: Do you have to work with the whole dream or only a
part?

ARNY: You should do whatever you like. You can start with any
part of the dream, with any signal, with a dream figure, an eye
movement, pain, relationship problem or whatever. All signals
are useful starting points. They are all streams leading to the
same river.

People turn to each other in pairs and begin to work on their
dreams. After about ten minutes Arny begins to talk again.

ARNY: If you are really open to the way people do dreamwork,
you can work with anybody. I remember working with a child
once who was three and she had a dream. Here's how she told
it. She said, "No, I do not dream, except sometimes." And I
said, "Sometimes? Some dreams?" And she said, "Those
dreams come from my mattress."

Everyone around the room laughs.

So, what are you going to do with a mattress? I said, "Your
dreams are in your mattress?" "Yeah," she said, "I only dream
when my mattress is here." So thinking that kids like to play, I
picked up a pillow from the floor. She said immediately, "Yes,

a dream could be in there." And I said, "Well, how do you get to it?"

"You squeeze it," she said. "If you squeeze it, a little dream would come out bit by bit." So here was a very special form of dreamwork! Everyone has his own very, very special way, especially little kids. I first squeezed the pillow and then the little girl did too. And then I even gave her a gentle squeeze and to my surprise, she cried and all sorts of sweet and bitter things came out of her through her tears. Everyone has their own dreamwork.

LAURA: How does this work connect to the archetypes?

ARNY: Do you mean how does process work connect to Jungian analysis?

Laura nods.

Analysts usually are not trained to pick up signals or feedback. Most focus on the content, not the process of the dream. On the other hand, many process workers neglect symbolism. Jungians say that way down deep, all archetypes are contaminated. What they mean is that when you get into the images, they begin to flow. They call that flow and mixture the collective unconscious. This is what I am calling process. What Jung called the Self reveals itself dynamically in the processes we are working with.

But there's a close connection between analysts and process workers. A classical analyst or ordinary psychotherapist interprets or advises, while a process worker helps the individual dreamer to unfold meaning herself. Obviously a good analyst would help life to unfold, and the best process worker would also know how to use a flowing interpretation, one which pulls present and past experience together.

MARTHA: What would a process interpretation be like?

ARNY: With my dream it might b, "Notice your fire and excitement and the conflict you have with it, and then become aware of a centering process."

MARTHA: Do you think dreams show the way?

ARNY: All I know for sure is that dreams are the pictures of states
waiting to turn into processes. Dreams are maps of the beginning of an otherwise uncharted trip into the unknown. They
are pictures of the unknown which appear in many channels.
Because process work is body-oriented, I put a stress upon
feelings, but dreams are not pictures of just feelings; they are
pictures of the way the unknown is showing itself in a given
moment.

Thus I do not focus upon images as if they were cookie
cutters which describe or create the person, but the awareness
of them and their changes. During our work if fire comes up,
we look and think about fire, but also work with the experience behind it. I may even drop the image, working with the
movement and noticing how body feeling creates something
new. Then your individual process might go on to new
images.

The basic idea is that I do not stick closely to images as the
main channel for everyone because this can inadvertently fix
you into a state where you begin to understand yourself in
terms of one image instead of the movement and energy of life
which created that image.

I understand typology, too, as only a small part of the person.' I listen to how people identify themselves as being
women or men, African, Asian, European, etc., and try to
appreciate that. But in her heart, the process worker does not
identify the client only with what he or she is saying at the
moment.

This is a political platform. I do not focus upon your being
solely American or African, black or Asian, male or female,
but upon your changing experience of yourself and your
awareness of that. This is a process experience of yourself and
your awareness of that. This is a process attitude towards
democracy; I call it deep democracy. I focus upon the process
between us as well as the differences between our identities.

I hate to get carried away at this point, but there has always
been something very important for me here, something spiritual. We are neither this nor that; we are a body which is in

the midst of change and evaporating. We are timeless, thousands of years old, and involved with processes which go beyond our present identity. This gives us an eternal feeling but one which is realizable right here in the moment.

Everyone becomes quiet for a moment.

CHAPTER 3

Edges and Altered States

T   he first evening of the seminar continues. Arny begins to discuss one of the central concepts of process work, the edge.

ARNY: I want to talk to you about edges. An edge is a filter to what you are perceiving. It marks the limits of who you are and what you imagine yourself capable of. It describes your capacities in a particular channel at a given moment.

Edges are a core issue in working with yourself because when you come to an edge, you lose your perceptions. You suspect, you even somehow know, that some signal or some feeling is there, but for some reason, you cannot let it in. You get confused. You know something's there, but you don't seem to be fully aware of it. You have to ask again and again what's happening. You forget things, and get embarrassed and mixed up at the edge.

Maybe I can explain this to you more rapidly by asking you to experience it.

Identifying the Edge

Ask yourself if there's something that you want to do but cannot yet do. Take a moment and reflect on something in your
life that you could possibly do, but that you're not quite doing.
See if you can get into contact with it. Think of something in
your life that you are almost able to do, you could do it, you
are capable of doing it; in fact, you do it occasionally or have
done it. You can even imagine doing it, but it doesn't come
easily. You feel it would be difficult to do; you are blocked
from doing it. Can you imagine that? Does anyone have difficulty connecting to such an edge? A growing edge? Maybe
this diagram will be helpful. Here's the edge. [*Goes to the blackboard and draws the diagram below.*]

Would somebody give me an example? What sort of edges
are you thinking about?

PAM: I'm thinking about promoting myself.

ARNY: If you could, how would you promote yourself?

PAM: I'm thinking of developing a program, of developing a
whole series of talks.

ARNY: OK. Promoting yourself. [*To the group*] Now one of the
things about an edge is that it represents a really huge identity
crisis. On the right side, let us say, is a new identity. On the left
side is an old identity. [*To Pam*] Who is the person in you who
can't promote herself? How do you identify yourself most of
the time? What kind of person would you say you are?

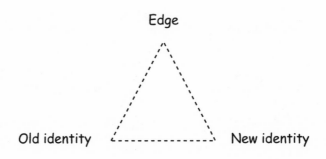

The edge

PAM: Well, in the past I was brought up to live under a bushel basket. It was dangerous to be seen.

ARNY: Yes, not to be seen. And what did you say? What kind of person did you say you were? What did you say about a basket? You said you were living under a basket?

PAM: Yeah, I was hiding my life under a basket.

Arny turns to the blackboard and writes "Being seen," to the right. He draws a basket to the left of the triangle, and says

ARNY [*To Pam*]: On the left is the person who was sitting under the basket. That was an identity that you used to have and which is still hanging on to you. And this new person on the other side, who can be seen when the basket isn't there, is a new identity.

These edges are really important. One of the reasons you can't promote yourself is because your whole identity as a person is called into question. The edge protects and conserves your old identity. Making that identity change isn't very simple; it usually involves a huge crisis.

[*To the group*] There are all sorts of methods for getting across that edge. Most of the methods involve changing channels and using channel theory. [*To Pam*] For example, have you ever seen anyone, or dreamed about someone who can be seen easily? Have you ever known someone who can be seen easily, can step out and doesn't hide under a basket?

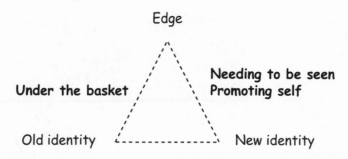

Pam's edge

PAM: I'm not sure. Nobody comes to mind right now.

ARNY: Nobody comes to mind right now. Have you ever dreamed about anybody like that?

PAM: I just had a dream last night or this morning actually.

ARNY: Yes, of course!

PAM: In the dream there was this whole group of people. Each one of them got up and did something different. I was very surprised that in this graduating class each person did something different.

ARNY: In front of the group?

PAM: In front of the group. Ah! And they prepared it ahead of time. [*She laughs.*] That's exactly what I told you I would like to do!

ARNY: And they each showed themselves!

PAM: Yeah!

ARNY: Yes, the dream got over the edge. Now you helped me to explain something I was just going to say; namely, that most of our dreams occur over the edge. Dreams are pictures of states trying to happen. [*Pointing to the right side of the diagram*] Here, on the other side of the edge, is where you are dreaming! You are not just dreaming in a random way. Your dreams are highly organized by your edges. We rarely dream directly about the edge itself, but usually dream over the edge.

[*To the group*] You see, in Pam's dreams people are already over the edge doing what they need to, showing themselves, being visible. Thus, asking about dreams is a method of going over edges.

I promise to use as little technical vocabulary as possible. But we shall need the term "primary process" to describe the state of hiding under the basket. The primary process is the state or way you identify yourself, and the secondary process is how we describe the behavior on the other side, the behavior that is connected to the new identity.

Your body symptoms all occur in the battleground between the identities. They are part of the edge phenomenon. If you want to create a body symptom, by the way, the thing to do is to reach an edge and not go over it. It's the shortest way of getting sick if you want to try it. Of course, we're all trying it all the time!

Since we now know the program for getting sick, we also know how to get well. All we have to do, in principle, is reverse the program. Instead of staying behind the edge we have to go over it.

Getting over the Edge

There are many ways of getting over the edge. If we think of the edge as a bridge, one way to cross that bridge is to imagine or dream ourselves over to the other side. But dreaming alone does not always succeed because it is done in an altered state. Consciously visualizing is a better way to do it.

Another way to get over an edge is to imagine a figure preventing you from your new identity and then battling this figure who resides at the edge. This figure personifies the ways in which we inhibit ourselves, the philosophies by which we have been living until now. This figure implies things like "Be nice to everyone," "Do not be cold," or "Don't be too emotional." "Love your neighbor instead of yourself." "Adults are good; kids are childish." You know, things like, "Hiding under baskets is good; being seen is bad."

One method for going over edges, a method Amy and I learned from two African witch doctors this summer, is to let the witch doctor deal with the edge figure. Now the witch doctors we just saw in Africa do not focus primarily upon the new identity on the other side of the edge, upon the new development which is trying to happen. Instead, they focus upon the demon on the bridge, the edge figure itself.

The most potent witchcraft works on problems by attacking the edge figure. Witch doctors describe the edge figure as the person who is jealous of you and wants to destroy you. They work on relationship problems, body problems, mental illness and ghosts by imagining the people who hate you. These jealous people are the demons at the bridge, the edge figures keeping you from your total self.

The witch doctors have visions of this spirit or person who is voodooing your life and holding up your development. In their visions they "see" the jealous figure who wants to hold you back. The jealous figure doesn't want you to change because then you would get ahead and make him or her even more jealous. These jealous demons usually have a philosophy which would be disturbed by your new developments.

These figures depress you with their philosophy. They deem the new, secondary processes unacceptable and filter out the information of the new identity. Thus, you cannot live your secondary identity consciously as part of your everyday life and it has to live at the outskirts of your awareness. The information is stored, so to speak, in your body as symptoms, in your dreams or in the relationship conflicts surrounding you.

Let's try the experiment now. As I'm speaking, imagine someone who is against you. Imagine someone who doesn't like you much or who once wanted to hurt you. Can you imagine how they could personify your own resistances against the new identity? [*Pauses, giving the group a chance to imagine the edge figures.*]

Now, the witch doctor tries to reverse the effect this figure has on you by using magic. I advise you to try to reverse the effect by reversing what is happening inside of you. Instead of fighting the figure, experiment with taking its side! Go ahead and do that now, for a moment, as an imagination. Take its side in an inner dialogue and tell yourself that you must not change. Notice all the different responses and experiences which happen.

This figure personifies feelings you have against yourself. Some of these feelings are useful criticisms, but most of these feelings are probably invalid. The figure frequently turns out to be a side of yourself which also wants to develop but is stuck. For example, a woman who wanted to go into business was held back by an idea that she had to mother her children. This idea or figure, whom she felt to be like her own mother, was just a bit too sentimental. After all, her kids were already grown up! The mother is her own behavior which is stuck on mothering. It might have been meaningful when the kids were little, but not now. She needed to reverse the effect of the edge figure by getting the mother to go into business too!

So go ahead and meet the inner edge figure. Listen to its criticism and check out whether or not it is a part of your own present behavior which wants to change.

The witch doctor bumps off the edge figure in her own way. I prefer to deal with the figure inwardly and to talk to it about its reasons for keeping me back.

JIM: I'm not quite sure what you mean when you say that dreams are over the edge.

ARNY: The dreams that you have are about another identity that is trying to happen, but isn't quite here yet. Pam is shy about being seen. The dreams that she had last night about people getting up and showing themselves are over her edge. The people are doing what she cannot: showing themselves and being seen.

JIM: So would that be similar to a wish fulfillment?

ARNY: Yes. Maybe one of the reasons Freud said that some dreams are wish fulfillments is because in dreams you are able to do things that you would probably like to do in a waking state.

JIM: How do you work in practice on the edge?

ARNY: The way to work on the edge in practice is utterly individual. Sometimes people just need courage to go over edges. Sometimes they need to have an inner dialogue with the edge figure. Sometimes process work merely points out the edge. I tell people to notice that they are at an edge, that they are changing subjects, going back to an old identity, going unconscious and forgetting what they were talking about. I simply tell them to notice it happening, and notice how they feel about it.

We do not just follow the continuum of the client's awareness. We do not follow everything the client notices, all the signals and behavior of the client. The process worker intervenes, helping the client to notice that at certain moments a secondary process, a new identity, is about to appear. At that point, where a secondary process appears, the client can choose, of course, whether she wants to become aware of it or not.

JANET: Oh, that is different than some forms of Gestalt therapy, which by and large follows the awareness the client chooses.

ARNY: Really? We differentiate between primary, secondary and edge behavior. We're aware of edges and give the client the option to go over them or not.

JANET: Is the goal in the working through the edge to get to the other side?

ARNY: Everyone's goal is different because we all have such different processes. One of my goals is to be aware of what happens at the edges.

Your development usually doesn't go in a linear way. It takes a more circular route, going over the edge a bit, then back, then over again, and then it might sit in the middle for a while.

One of the reasons I don't push people over the edge to make them have a breakthrough is because I always try to take the path of least resistance. I'm a bit lazy and take the minimalist's approach to therapy these days. But a more important reason is that most clients resist going over edges because they do not yet have enough information about how to live on the other side. The new identity and behavior may not yet be formed; it takes time to create new patterns.

Let's say I'm a person who is very shy and on the other side of my shyness is aggression. The only person I ever saw who was aggressive was a relative whom I hated. Let's pretend even further that you act like a great therapist and push me over the edge. Therapists tend to want their clients to make radical changes. So let's say that you want to be a good therapist and press me over my edge and suddenly I become aggressive.

You have a momentary success and I say, "Thank you. Finally I can be aggressive." I go back home and go over all my edges. I am nasty to everyone and inadvertently lose my job and make enemies. Of course, that could be good. But something is missing: patience. The reason I vacillated at the edge in the first place was that I didn't know how to handle the relationship issues which would come up once I became aggressive. So I asked you to help me be aggressive. You helped me do it. I did it, but then decided that therapy with you is not for me, because it made me lose my job.

This is why I don't push for cathartic breakthroughs. I try to go slowly and gently. Things happen too rapidly for me anyway. Wait and see. When you have a full pattern of how to live with your new identity, you will make the necessary change in two seconds. If Pam really promotes herself and becomes successful, she will then have a whole other world of things to do that she may not yet be thinking of.

I am really happy I didn't know how to promote myself years ago because I would not have been able to handle the onslaught of recognition and mail which I've experienced in the last years. And even now I'm just barely up to it.

So please consider breakthroughs momentary ecstasies and don't forget to appreciate and support all the tough, slow work that's needed to build up to the new identity.

Altered States, Magic and the Unoccupied Channel

I want to talk about altered states for a moment and then demonstrate how to work with them. There are many ways of talking about altered states. [*Arny goes to the board again and draws a diagram of the edge and altered states.*]

Altered states occur when, for one reason or another, our process takes us over the edge. In that moment we get a brief experience of what's in the dreaming world over here. [*He points to the right side of the diagram.*] Perhaps the most useful way of getting across the edge is by working with those altered states, bringing them into awareness, and helping them to unfold. Let me explain, then we can practice working with altered states.

Altered states happen in our unoccupied channels. A channel is "occupied" when the person identifies with the

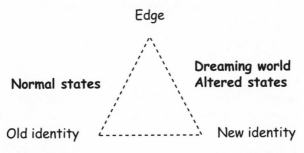

The edge and the altered states

event taking place in that channel. One cue that we have for detecting whether or not a channel is occupied is by the way people speak. If people use the word "I" with a particular action, we say that action, and hence channel, is occupied. For example, "I sing" or "I talk a lot" are occupied auditory experiences.

On the other hand, "They were listening to music" means that listening to music is, in the moment, not done by you, by the "I" you identify yourself with. Thus, auditory experiences are now unoccupied; they occur to unknown or rejected parts of you. If I therefore ask you to get into the auditory channel and sing the first tune that comes into your head, this will create an altered state. Performing an activity in an unoccupied channel creates feelings and states that are outside your normal identity. You feel "stoned," "euphoric" or "tranced out."

Movement is one of the least occupied channels for people all over the world. We all make many movements but few of them are occupied consciously by our identity. Therefore we cannot retrace these movements. Only a small percentage of our movements are congruent with what we are doing, thinking and saying. Watch me as I move and try to find my unoccupied movements, ones that aren't congruent with what I am doing or saying.

[*Arny takes his glasses off and begins to make a variety of movements, but suddenly stops.*] Wait a minute. What did I just do with my glasses? Was that movement occupied? Do you think it was occupied?

[*He puts his glasses back on and tries to recall the movements that he made.*] Now, what was that? I swear I did it unconsciously. I'm new to glasses. I had glasses earlier in my life, but after working with my eyes, I decided not to wear them anymore. But now I'm wearing them again, and, boy, they drive me crazy!

[*Arny takes his glasses off again, but more slowly and consciously. He puts them on and takes them off again.*] Actually, taking them off is the beginning of throwing them away! Now that would be difficult, being nearsighted and staying with what's inside of me! What an edge! [*He giggles and looks shyly at the group.*]

Yes, taking off those glasses was an unoccupied motion. Isn't that amazing? It looks from the outside as if I'm identifying with taking them off, but it's a very unconscious business and it would be very helpful to work on myself by actually throwing them out.

An Example of Working with Unoccupied Movement

Let me give you an example with somebody else. I'd like to talk to somebody about a problem they are having. Would somebody work with me for a few minutes?

A middle-aged man in the group volunteers to work. Arny comes toward him and says, "Hello. I forgot your name. What is it?" The man says his name is Eric.

ARNY: Right, Eric. What sort of stuff have you been working on in yourself?

ERIC: I've been working on being more assertive and more active in making money, and putting myself forward.

ARNY: Putting yourself forward is hard to do? Can you tell me something more about yourself? What I'm doing with you is listening for the channels which are unoccupied. Could you say something about yourself?

ERIC: Well, at the moment I am feeling very awkward and self-conscious.

Arny notes to himself that by coupling the verb "feeling" with "I," Eric identifies with proprioception, or inner body feeling. Thus, proprioception is an occupied channel.

> I tend to underestimate myself a lot, though I can do a number of things very well. I am very good in relationship in terms of understanding clinically.

Here Eric is also identifying with his actions in relationships. Thus, the relationship channel is occupied.

> I'm good at music and singing.

Singing and music are auditory phenomena. He's identifying with his abilities and thus the auditory channel is occupied.

> I love people, I have a lot of fun, at least with some people. I'm scared of strangers and groups a lot of times, but with people I know I can be very free and alive.

ARNY: Mhhm. And what sort of things happen to you?

ERIC: What things seem to happen to me? Well, I come to the end of the month and I don't have enough money to pay the bills. At the end of the year I underestimate my taxes. The car breaks down and I need thousands of dollars to repair it but I don't have the money. It seems like there's a blind spot there. And every year I say I'm going to get this organized and it's not going to happen again but it happens again. So I get to feeling foolish and inadequate and powerless about that.

One participant comments on how Eric uses his hands as he speaks and guesses that he is in the kinesthetic channel. Arny then asks the participant if Eric uses his hands consciously or unconsciously. The participant replies, "Unconsciously."

ARNY: Yes, unconsciously. He's not quite doing it consciously because he does not complete his movements. And he describes his problems as "trouble putting himself forward," and his car breaks down.

> [*To the group*] For Eric, movement is problematical. He does not organize it; it does things to him. It operates almost randomly. Thus, since movement is not occupied and since I

want to do an exercise on altered states, I will choose to work with his edge of not being able to assert himself by working with movement.

[*To Eric*] I wonder if you would like to work with me for a minute. OK?

Eric agrees. Arny walks over to where Eric is sitting in the circle, and reaches out his hand.

OK, this is going to be very easy. All you have to do is stand up.

Eric stands up and they both walk towards the middle of the circle. Arny says to Eric as they stand there, "Now there's not much more to do except to notice what is happening now." They stand facing one another. Arny has his hands in his pockets. In a very nonchalant manner he says to Eric, "Hi." Eric readjusts his shoulders ever so slightly, pulling them backwards as his chest comes forward a tiny bit.

I just noticed a little movement. There it is. Yeah, would you do that again?

Shoulders back

Arny shows Eric the movement he made. Then he faces him and gently touches his shoulders to help him find the movement again. Eric repeats the motion.

> Yeah that's it. Go ahead and do it, really do it and amplify it a tiny bit. This time take your time, Eric. Put your shoulders back like that and hold it for just a minute.

Eric repeats the motion and stops when his shoulders are back and his chest is jutting forward.

> That's right. Now tell me, what is the difference between having your shoulders back like that and the way you were before?

Eric tries his original posture again. He stands with slumped shoulders and his arms hang at his sides. Then he tries the other posture. He pulls his shoulders back and juts his chest forward.

ERIC: Well, in the first one, I feel weak. And with my shoulders back, I feel open.

ARNY: You feel open. What is the feeling difference that would go along with your overall behavior if you put your shoulders back like that?

ERIC: Well, ah, I think I'd feel powerful and would be more assertive!

Slumped posture

The group is fascinated by Eric's discovery and starts to make comments, nodding and indicating that they understand what's happening.

ARNY [*To the group*]: Any unoccupied movement done unintentionally, like that shoulder movement, is the thing we are looking for. Movement, here the unoccupied channel, has the solution. Assertiveness and putting himself forward is an altered state, the dreaming process on the other side of the edge. To find it takes only a second. It's right over the edge. [*To Eric*] You said you have trouble putting yourself forward, but there it is in your body, in your movements, in the way you stick out your chest.

ERIC [*Excitedly*]: It's also in my chin. [*He moves his chin in and out.*]

ARNY: It's in there, too, yeah. Let's go on with the movement you made at the beginning of putting your shoulders back and chest out.

Eric does it right away, this time with even more strength. He announces to all how terrific it feels.

ARNY: Doesn't it feel great? So that is over the edge to do something like that. It doesn't go along with your normal identity. So let's pretend this is going to be a new identity, whatever it is, with your shoulders back like that.

Arny goes behind him and pulls his shoulders back a bit. He then puts a hand on Eric's chest to help him feel himself more. Eric begins to beam, enjoying this new posture.

Great. Do you want to make a couple of steps that seem congruent with this particular posture? Let's take a walk around together.

Eric and Arny both begin to walk around with their shoulders back and their chests forward.

ERIC: This is a little weird. Well, I can imagine doing this by myself, but not in front of all these people!

Everyone laughs.

ARNY: Yes, you can imagine doing this by yourself.

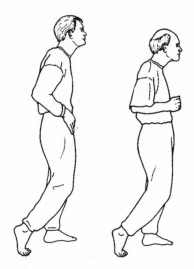

Strutting around

ERIC: I don't know. I can hardly imagine strutting around like this.

ARNY: It's unimaginable doing it in front of all these people? You can't identify with your new identity. [*Arny looks around, scratches his head.*] How did we get into this? We're outside of the imagination. It's hard to imagine this. But can you?

Eric says that he can imagine it. His statement that he can imagine doing it alone indicates that the visual channel is more occupied than movement. Arny is now taking the new information about assertiveness from an unoccupied channel and putting it into an occupied one, visualization.

Try to imagine it, and tell me your imagination while you are doing it. I'll try to help you.

They both begin to walk again. Eric walks with his chest out further and shoulders back, looking proud and strong.

ERIC: What do I imagine? Well, I imagine being a rooster with feathers. [*He makes a movement with his hands, indicating feathers behind him. He starts to strut around the room, like a rooster, and*

Proud rooster

then stops. He giggles and looks around.] I can't do it. That's all I can do.

ARNY [*Jokingly*]: It's an edge. You can walk with slumped shoulders, but not like a rooster. [*Arny starts to mirror him, showing him his original slumped posture and then the new posture, with his chest out and shoulders back.*] Well, maybe it's time to go back to the original posture.

Arny slumps over and the two of them shuffle around the room with their shoulders slumped forward. After a few minutes, Eric pulls his shoulders back and says defiantly, "I'd rather stick my chest out!"

ARNY: You'd rather do this? Sure you would. I can believe it. Why did you make that choice?

ERIC: It feels better, except I keep hearing my mother saying, "Don't be too proud."

ARNY: OK, just stay here for a minute. [*Arny leaves Eric and walks over to the triangle diagram on the blackboard. He turns to the whole group.*] So here we have pride and assertiveness on the right

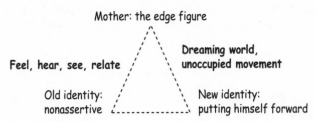

Eric's edge

side of the triangle. Who stands here at the edge, in between Eric's new and old identities?

From across the room, Eric says in a loud, booming voice, "Who stands there? My mother!"

ARNY: Right. How could we go on working with this if we were to process this in detail? We went over the edge and now an inner figure, his mother, connected with the old identity is pulling him back.

   [*Arny turns to Eric.*] Your mother is saying, "Don't be proud." Is that right?

Eric nods.

   Do you hear her?

Eric nods.

   Out of which ear do you hear her?

Eric points to his right ear. Arny walks over to him and stands on his right side. "How far away is she?" Eric indicates that she's very close. He points to a spot just above and behind his right ear. Arny walks over to that spot, but before he can get there, Eric shrugs his shoulders and walks away. Arny follows him and everyone laughs.

ARNY [*Apologetically to Eric*]: Please excuse me for coming back to that awful position again. But let's say, just for a moment, there was somebody here. [*He goes back to the position behind Eric and speaks in a falsetto.*] Now, Eric, you shouldn't do that. Don't act proud!

Eric doesn't move, but suddenly pulls his shoulders back, turns to Arny and says, "Forget it!"

ARNY [*Continuing to play the role of the mother*]: Eric, what are you talking about? You don't normally talk to me like that!

Eric walks up to Arny and slaps the "mother" on the shoulders. Arny begins to collapse out of the mother's role.

ERIC [*To Arny*]: Right. Who wants to be normal?!

ARNY [*In a much weaker voice*]: You don't want to be...

ERIC [*Interrupts*]: No. Not your way. I'm going to do it my way.

ARNY [*Turns to the group*]: It's difficult now for me to go on playing that role, Can you understand why? I can't do it. He did something that makes it impossible for me to do that, and he did it very well.

One of the participants answers Arny's question by making the slapping motion that Eric made to the mother, and says, "Yeah, he lowered you."

ARNY: Yes, Eric did something very strong and congruent. He knocked me out of that role so it's no longer organic for me to play that part. If I were to go on playing it, it would be a game. It wouldn't be congruent with the way I'm feeling any more. When you play a role make sure that you watch what people do. If they change your feelings, they have changed theirs as well.

  Eric, that was really strong what you did to my shoulder. I felt that you really did something. Shall we go back and test that? [*Eric shakes his head.*] OK. That's the end for now.

Eric tells Arny that he feels finished. They both go back to their places in the circle and sit down.

ARNY: All the things we want to do are right there in the unoccupied channels. Whenever you get into an unoccupied channel, soon enough the figure at the edge comes up, and we wander back and forth between normal and altered states. Then, when the edge figure is relieved of its job, everything is ready, and we begin to change identity.

When Eric stood up, he made this particular motion [*Arny pulls his shoulders back*] and then he stopped. One of the characteristics of an unoccupied motion is that it doesn't complete itself. We couldn't exactly tell what the message in the movement was. It looked like he was a bit stiff, like most people. You can tell something is unoccupied because the message in the channel is unclear.

JOAN: Could you have worked another way?

ARNY: There are many, many ways of beginning process work. None of them are right or wrong. They depend upon your creativity and the client's feedback. One of them has to do with listening carefully to what people say and determining how to work from that. You can also use your eyes and see secondary processes and work with them directly through movement. Those of you gifted with your hands can pick up signals and channels just through your fingertips. Those who are mediumistic pick up information through internal channels. There are many places to enter the stream.

You see, if you miss one signal, that's OK. You don't have to process every signal. Important signals repeat themselves. In fact, one signal usually connects to all the other secondary signals, because each signal is part of a greater message. The message comes through if you process any one signal completely. It's not simply the individual signals which fascinate us; it is the larger global message which they lead us to.

Thus, you might work with the shoulder motion or the chin. A typical analyst would have focused on the mother. Dream workers would have looked into the visions and imaginations. There is not one right way of doing it.

ANNIE: Why do you call working with the unoccupied channel "dreaming"?

ARNY: If you listen to the way people talk and notice the channels they are not occupying, you can guess their dreams! Try it with your roommate tonight. Try discovering the unoccupied material and guess what the person is dreaming about. Your roommate will think you are a mind reader! But it's not ordinary magic at all. It is the scientific core of information and psychology.

TESS: You seem to imply that it's important not to do too much at any one time. You just stay with one simple signal, one unoccupied channel and amplify that.

ARNY: Yes, that's because my father told me that it's very important to do as little as possible and to enjoy your life! So let's say that's enough for this evening and meet tomorrow morning.

The group applauds and people slowly begin to leave the room. Some remain talking and gossiping about the evening, and others slowly wander out into the California night.

PART II

Individual Work

CHAPTER 4

Meditation

E arly the next morning, after breakfast, we all return to Huxley fresh and eager to go.

ARNY: This morning I'd like to give you an experience of process work done by you alone. Paradoxically, the better the therapist, the greater the client's need for working independently on herself alone. The better you are, the more dangerous you could be for the client. If you are a really good therapist and thus extremely helpful to people, at a certain point you become ineffective because the client's awareness becomes projected onto you.

This is how I view inner work. If you are invited to a foreign country to do conflict resolution, you are wisest if you help that country as much as possible, and then either leave immediately or stay a bit longer to teach them how to do the work for themselves. The same is true if an individual asks you for help.

Now, how can you give your awareness of the individual back to her? Loving you as a therapist is important, but she will appreciate you even more if you slowly assist her in her own inner work. One way of giving back process-oriented psychology to a client is through inner work awareness procedures.

I was talking on the telephone the other day to a publisher who was reading my manuscript on inner work and he said, "For Godsakes, tell me, is it psychology?" And I said, "No, not really." "Is it meditation?" he asked, and I laughed and said, "No, no." Then he asked, "Well, what is it?" And I said, "It is neither psychology nor meditation: it's process work." And I continued, "Both meditation and psychology evolve out of each other. If you need to appreciate and become aware of what's happening to you, then inner work is a form of psychology. But if you need to let things go through you, then inner work is a form of meditation."

The Irreducible

The basic focus this morning is to become aware of the irreducible element in your experience. Now let me explain what I mean. Something is irreducible when you can't dissect it further into its parts without destroying it. That's important. Let's take a movement, for example. If I reduce a movement down to one small motion, I might lose the overall process. Thus, the entire movement is the irreducible process, and not the components that make it up.

Or, in another example, let's say that I catch myself looking up, and after working on it, I have a sense that it's an attempt to connect to a god above me. That is a very strong experience. If you then tell me at that moment to reduce that process even further by listening to God, or by feeling it somewhere inside, or by focusing on my arm movements, that would ruin the process. It would reduce it to its components and I would lose the meaning. We can therefore say that the process is irreducible.

Thus, inner work begins by asking yourself elementary questions about the irreducible sensory-grounded elements, or channels. To begin then, let's find the irreducible element of our focus. You need only become aware of what you are aware of. If you do not know immediately, then just ask yourself if you are seeing, hearing, moving, relating or feeling. That is all you have to do.

To practice and to sharpen your awareness we shall begin with noticing seeing, hearing, and feeling. Why don't we just try that for a little bit? Let's work internally for five minutes. Find a comfortable spot. The less you move to begin with, the better off you are.

Some people sit and others lie down. Arny begins to speak in a slow and soft tone. He uses this meditative voice in order not to disturb the internal work of the participants, and also to meditate on what he is doing.

Meditation consists of one question. Are you seeing something, are you hearing something or are you feeling something? These are generally irreducible sensory signals. Let's work with these three channels. Do you hear, feel or see? Simply notice which channel you are in. That's the work. That is all for the moment. Then I'll start talking in about five minutes.

Everyone meditates deeply on the question. The room is silent. Five minutes go by. Arny begins to speak in a quiet, slow voice.

When you open your eyes, I'll know that you are ready to go on to the next step.

People begin to open their eyes and look up.

Now, let me ask you a really funny question. Do you have any idea what you are doing when you are not meditating, when you are not aware of your awareness? What are you doing when you are not aware of the kinds of perceptions that you're having?

Most people create their primary process when they are not meditating. When you are not meditating, you are sort of on "cruise control," unconsciously following a program called, "fulfilling your identity and doing the things that identify you as so-and-so." The inner work procedure we're doing now helps you become aware of that and also helps you pick up things that are very secondary. If you do not work on yourself, then you operate in what Charles Tart would call a consensus hypnosis, unconsciously fulfilling impersonal cultural tasks and goals.

By the way, working with your own sensory-grounded experiences is not just inner work that you can use on yourself but is also very useful when working with withdrawn clients, people in catatonic or comatose states, or kids who don't talk much. Just ask them to focus internally and follow their own flow of perceptions, their own channel awareness.

Amplifying

Now what I'd like you to do is easy. I'm going to say it first and then we'll do it. What I'd like you to do is not only catch the channel—whether you are seeing, hearing or feeling something inside—but amplify the experiences that you are having in the channel that they occur. Let's take feeling, for example. What sort of things did you feel in your body?

Arny turns to a participant nearby, and she answers, "My pulse, breathing." Arny turns to the others and asks, "How could she amplify that?" Another participant suggests that she amplify it by breathing.

Yes, by breathing, by becoming aware of the entire process of breathing. Feel your pulse in your chest. You might want to feel the pulse in your fingertips and neck. Take the experience and amplify it further proprioceptively.

If you are tired or have a bellyache, take the experiences you have in your stomach or chest and, for example, increase them spatially. This is a very useful way of working with your body feelings. Take a localized feeling and generalize it. Let it take up more space in your body until you become that feeling. That's a way to integrate a local body experience.

Working with Menstrual Cramps

A woman named Lisa turns to Arny and asks: "May I ask you a question about a process I just did?"

ARNY: Sure.

LISA: I had menstrual cramps, and I hadn't expected that. I started to feel the cramps all over my body. They pulsed, and then the pulse turned into seeing the ocean. I heard the ocean and then started thinking about the waves, you know, that I saw this morning...

ARNY [*Interrupts*]: How did you know that you started thinking about the waves?

LISA: I heard them. Is that switching from one channel, feeling, into another, hearing?

Arny nods.

But still my body went into waves.

ARNY [*Nods*]: Yes, into movement. You did the channel switching I wanted to teach later. Go on.

LISA: So then I started thinking about the waves and then I felt my body pulsing, like waves coming into shore. The waves came up and down, pulsing, and then it seemed to switch into the visual channel. I was looking at someone's breath, and then I started to cry, because it was the picture of a friend as he was dying.

ARNY: Mhmm. You were switching channels and I'm glad that you could follow that happening. Then, apparently, something irreducible happened. From the elementary pulsing, the waves and the water, you remembered your friend's dying breaths.

LISA: What happened is that the wave turned into his or my body, and that's when the picture hit me. It must have been an edge because I was glad when the exercise was over. What I was trying to do was to see exactly what I was to do next.

ARNY: Go ahead now. Meditate and see if you can connect with that person who died. See if you can go on and visualize him. Maybe you can see him in life and observe where your inner perceptions go next. Or perhaps you will want to experiment with being him and knowing the part of you which is trying to die. Or maybe you can find out how you are like him, or might need to be like him in your own life.

DAVE: Shouldn't she be integrating that person in her everyday life? Sometimes, they say, grieving is relieved by integrating.

ARNY: Yes, of course. But what does "integrate" mean, and what is everyday life? Each of us has another meaning for these terms. The most powerful and safest form of integration is for the meditator to experience that part of herself now, right in the moment. This immediate and momentary awareness is a form of integration more powerful than translating an insight into a future form of behavior. We must follow her. If she begins to focus on memories and visions of her everyday life, then the vision called everyday life is where she will have to work.

[*To the group*] So, she had menstrual cramps. She just followed the flow of things. This time I want you to follow the flow of things and slow them down a bit by amplifying them as they come up. Let's say you're seeing something like the sea. What's a way of amplifying something visually?

PAM: Make it brighter.

ARNY: Make it brighter, or look more closely. See the forms more clearly and watch more intensely what's going on. And if you are hearing something? There are so many ways of amplifying an auditory signal. If it's a voice, ask yourself if it's a young or an old voice. Is it a male or a female voice? Hear it more clearly. Is it an animal or a human that you are hearing? Go into the details of what you are hearing.

The purpose of this work is to let the flow teach you about life and to be able to pick up what's happening in yourself and then use it. I think if Buddha were here—if he knew about these things—he would say it is a way of clearing things out inside of yourself very rapidly.

TOM: What if it's not a vision or a sound, but simply thoughts? How do you work with them?

ARNY: Thinking is a general term without sensory-grounded awareness. How do you know when you think?

Tom takes a moment and thinks about this question. As he thinks, his eyes move upward.

TOM: I think it's words and emotions that come up.

ARNY: That's interesting. When I asked you the question we could see the channel of thinking in your eye motion. [*To the group*] See if you can see what channel Tom is in when he does what he calls thinking. [*Turning to Tom again*] Find out again how you know when you're thinking, Tom.

This time Tom's eyes go directly to the side.

[*To the others*] Well, this time it changed. What was it this time? [*He demonstrates by repeating Tom's eye movements, casting his eyes to one side.*]

It looks like when you think, Tom, one thing you do is listen to words. You said before that thinking is "words." Neuro-linguistic practitioners point out that seeing, hearing, and feeling can be seen in the ways the eyes move. Looking upward frequently indicates seeing. Movement and feeling are often indicated by the eyes moving down, to the left or right. In addition, we have found that listening is often indicated by the eyes moving to the side, as if people are looking around or behind themselves. Visualizing can also be detected when people take sudden, deep breaths from their chests and then hold the breath slightly. Feeling can be noticed when the eyes flutter.

Thinking is one of the most hypnotic things that we do. We think without knowing how it is that we think. The majority of people think through audition: they are usually talking to themselves or to somebody else. Some people think visually: they see pictures relating to one another. And occasionally some people, often children, think proprioceptively: they think through their body experiences. Thus, instead of just thinking, ask yourself, "Am I seeing, hearing, feeling or moving?" You might notice, for instance, that thinking is a dialogue. Then you can work with it consciously.

Let's work for another five minutes. This time take the experiences that you're having and amplify them in the channel where they occur. Again, don't move much yet, because movement is also a way of distracting you from your proprioception.

Sit and keep your eyes closed for another couple of minutes. If you're hearing something, amplify the sound. If you're seeing something, see it more clearly. If you are feeling something in your body, feel it internally and amplify that body feeling. Let's do that for five minutes.

Five minutes pass. The participants seem to be intensely focused on their inner experiences. Slowly and quietly Arny speaks to the group and says, "When you open your eyes, I'll know you are ready to go on." After a minute or so, people start to open their eyes and look forward again. They have an introverted, meditative look about them.

WENDY: Arny, sometimes it seems like the channels are layered on top of each other.

ARNY: It is possible to be aware of three or more channels all at once. Usually these channels combine into one single experience which really cannot be reduced. They're so intertwined that you forget about the individual channels when you work with that larger experience.

WENDY: I find that it happens too fast. I start with a sensation or movement, but then something else comes, and again something else! It all seems so fast.

ARNY: You might want to work with the speed itself rather than any particular content. Why not experiment with the question, "Who needs this speed, and what does he need it for?"

SAM: One of the things that interferes with me—I'm not sure it's an interference—are comments that come to me while I'm feeling something proprioceptively.

ARNY: That's wonderful. Who makes the comments? Is it a male or a female voice?

SAM: Sometimes one, sometimes the other.

ARNY: OK. The next time you are feeling proprioceptively, connect to the commentator. Find out who's up there. Ask who's there. You might get the answer, "Well, I'm the voice of wisdom." Go on listening to that voice.

SAM: In this particular case I think the voice was male.

ARNY: You might work with that male voice using a channel change. This is what I want to recommend next.

Channel Switching

As we see from all of your experiences, channels change inside of you automatically and spontaneously. We can also use this automatic experience as an aid. If we let it happen spontaneously, it becomes the great disturber of all classical forms of meditation. But in process work the disturber is what we use as an intervention.

Channel changing is one of the best ways to increase and unfold experiences. It widens their dimensions, makes experiences more complete, fills them out and makes them global.

Instead of just letting channels change on their own, we are going to actually practice changing channels. For example, Sam, if I work with your experience, I would begin by listening to the inner commentator. Who is in there? I would dialogue with that inner figure and at a certain point switch channels and see the figure. I would look at the person who is talking and make an image out of that voice, to help the pattern to complete itself. I would then try feeling what it is like to be that voice. There's a feeling associated with the sound of the voice and with its image.

Most inner commentators are critics. And the majority of inner critics that I've met look like this. [*Arny sits up with a straight back, looks down, and points his finger in a judgmental way. Everyone giggles.*]

Sam, this figure may not be your process. I am taking off on your experience because it may help others with inner critics. If any of you has a critic, you might want to feel what it's like to be that critic. Even as I talk now, you can feel that critic. Feel what it is like to be inside the body of your critic. Now switch, and ask yourself where you feel that critic inside yourself. The answer to that question may be very humbling. Feel inside yourself where that critic lives in you.

Two Kinds of Awareness

Have you noticed that we are using two kinds of awareness at the same time? One awareness is diffuse and relaxed. It just hangs around and looks lazy, like a fisherman waiting for a bite. You act like you are drifting, and you look a little dumb.

The second kind of awareness is focused and precise. It is an exact awareness. You are sharp as a whip, intent and awake. These two kinds of awareness go perfectly together. If you are only intense and focused, you will not attract the fish you want to catch. If you are too relaxed, you will not notice the fish when it nibbles on your line! I often feel as if I am on vacation and relaxed, yet I am fully here and awake. Awareness notices everything, including itself! Your awareness observes you when you become diffuse and relaxed, as well as when you are intense and alert. Awareness notices how you move through different kinds of awareness.

So let's begin again. This time ask yourself again what channel you are in. Are you hearing, seeing or feeling? Then amplify your experiences in the channel where they are happening, but this time switch channels on your experiences. Build them out, fill them in and make them more global.

For example, if you are hearing the sea, look at the sea. Can you feel the sea inside of you physically? Can you move like the sea, make sounds like the sea, relate like the sea? This makes your experience very complete. Add other channels that were not there to begin with. Afterwards we'll work with movement. Try this channel changing for about ten minutes.

After ten minutes everyone is still intently involved in their work.

When you open your eyes I'll know that you are ready to go on. But as you open your eyes, notice your eye movements and follow the things that you look at first.

JOHN: That was a great experience. I've had pains in my back for a long time. When I lay down, the proprioceptive channel was open to me. I amplified the pain in my back and it moved down into my hip and toe and my hand, and I followed it around. Then, at one point, when it was in my hip, I changed to the auditory channel and asked my hip what it was saying. I heard two voices, two twelve-year-old kids in there, screaming and saying "Hey, let us out of here." So I asked, "Where do you want to go?" And they said, "We want [*He pauses and giggles*] to feel so-and-so's tits." It was suddenly elementary school and this girl was sitting there and...

ARNY [*Interrupts mischievously*]: And then?

John looks embarrassed and doesn't respond.

ARNY: That's a big edge!

Everyone laughs, including John.

JOHN: So then I followed the voice, and I wondered what else was going on. I realized that ah... hmm [*He giggles again*], what did I realize? [*He looks puzzled and a bit embarrassed.*]

ARNY [*With a smile*]: You realized that your wife is sitting next to you!

Everyone bursts into laughter again. Arny continues a bit more seriously.

Yeah, your pain became the kids who wanted to relate and feel more.

JOHN [*Chuckles*]: Yes, I started to feel bliss in my body and I realized that I was feeling pain and bliss the whole time. Where I was not feeling pain, I was actually feeling bliss. I amplified my experience. And then I said, "Give me some more information on this." And I heard a voice, a wise voice that said, "What you feel in your body as pain is incomplete experience.

I got the point. Pain was the beginning of the kids and the bliss. The pain just went away. I thought, "Oh, OK, I'll just process this need for tits and bliss" and I had no more pain!

HENRY: I have a question. Would you mind going back over primary and secondary meditation processes?

ARNY: While we are here in this room your primary meditation process will probably be trying to meditate, working on yourself and focusing internally. The secondary process for most meditators is almost always a disturbance. For example, a secondary process for people whose intention is to meditate would be sleepiness, noise, the telephone, a dog barking, another meditator burping, relationship problems. Does anyone know these problems?

Everyone laughs.

Can I talk to someone who is sleepy?

LISA: Actually, I'm usually very awake. In guided meditation, even when I have the intention to listen and follow, I suddenly realize that I am not following. I come back when the guide says to come back and I realize I was spaced out.

ARNY: Yeah. How do you know when you space out?

LISA: It's a quality of feeling; I just feel it.

ARNY: Notice Lisa's use of language. She said earlier that "she listens, follows or relates," indicating that relating and listening are occupied. Feeling is not occupied, since she describes her experience as "a quality of feeling." Her next statement, "I just feel," indicates that she can indeed occupy feeling, but doesn't when she spaces out. Noticing aspects of channels which are unoccupied is important because that is where we dream, get lost or go unconscious.

So here is a good example of going unconscious in an unoccupied channel. Feeling is probably unoccupied. So, Lisa, what does it feel like to space out? Let's pretend that you were now going to tell me how to space out. Could you tell me what to feel in order to space out?

LISA: Just float.

ARNY: OK. I'll try it and maybe when you or I get to the sleepy spot, I'll ask for more cues. OK, first I will space out by floating. [*He quietly experiences it.*] OK. I can do that.

LISA: And just let your thoughts go. Just let them float like a balloon.

ARNY: That's very helpful. I can let them float like a balloon. I can almost see the balloon now. I feel it moving. Can you see that balloon moving too?

Here Arny is helping her fill out the experience by switching from the proprioceptive to the visual channel.

LISA: It's red.

ARNY: A red balloon. And it's floating. I see it.

LISA: Let it go. It's a helium balloon.

ARNY [*Opens his eyes, puzzled*]: A *healing* balloon?

LISA: No, a *helium* balloon!

The people in the room giggle at Arny's mistake. Arny continues to follow her instructions and imagines into her experience. He tells her that he can no longer see the balloon.

LISA: You would probably be feeling spaced out.

ARNY: I am feeling spaced out, but I'm also seeing. How are you doing?

LISA: I feel very clear and light.

Everyone laughs because what she earlier described as spaced out, she now describes as clear and light.

ARNY: Sure, me too. I'm feeling and floating and I can see so brightly and clearly. Is there a tone that would go along with this brightness and clarity which you now see? Is there a tone you could make? Want to try it? Try it for a second.

LISA: I can hear it, but I don't know if I can make it.

ARNY: I'm sure you can't make it like you hear it. Try it though, even though it won't be exactly the same.

Lisa says she is scared of trying. Arny starts to experiment, making various high-pitched sounds by whistling. She tells him that it sounds like a high-pitched, synthesizer tone. She begins to make the sound like synthesized music, high and eerie. She is shocked by the sounds. She begins to cry, apparently touched by the sound she is hearing. The group listens quietly. After a minute of silence, Lisa thanks us and says no more.

ARNY: This is one way to process spacing out. For you, proprioception is not very occupied, thus you trip out on feeling. But if you follow that feeling and make pictures out of it, you see a balloon coming and going. Then there is the tone from this other world. There was an edge to experiencing that eeriness and apparent bliss. The channel switch to hearing helped to complete it.

Everyone gets fatigued and scared in an unoccupied channel. It's also possible just to get tired because of lack of sleep, or
because you don't have enough chance to relax. I have nothing
against sleeping if you need it. Why not sleep? But if you process a constant and predictable sleepiness, something new will
happen. Changing channels like we just did gives you another
view of things.

VIVIAN: I had an experience from the meditation we did a while
ago. What happened was first proprioception. I felt a band of
tension in my forehead and then I noticed it was also on the
top of my head. I switched channels and heard a voice say, "I
can be softened, softer, softer," and I just let it be softened. But
the headache remained.

ARNY: Perhaps the headache remained because the voice you
heard was *against* the proprioceptive experience. The voice
was not a new dimension of tension. It was not changing the
channel of the band of tension from proprioception to hearing. This voice you heard was your primary process. When
working with secondary experiences and channel changing,
be careful that the experience, when brought into a new channel, matches the theme of the experiences in other channels.

Your inner process will direct you better than I can from
the outside, but why not now feel the band of tension and
make a movement that is congruent with that band?

[*Arny waits a few minutes, while Vivian concentrates on feeling
the tension.*] Now make a movement that would be an expression of that band of tension. What movement would you
make?

Vivian makes a tense, grim-looking face.

That face! That's great. What a creative, super face! Please do
it again. Now that looks like a very real face. This time try
doing that face again, and if you can, make an inner picture of
what you are doing. Yeah, that's right. Make it again. Whose
face is that and what is it doing?

VIVIAN: Oh. It feels to me like a friend I know. Ah-hah!

ARNY [*To the group*]: Well, she got something. I will not follow the details or the content now, I just wanted to show how to use channel switching to get around an edge. Now you, Vivian, are further into meditation. Your movement and vision ampli-fied your headache feeling. Now you have a face that shocks you. Go on with that until you know all about that face, until you know what your friend wants and for what reasons. Try appreciating his or her viewpoint. Be him or her.

RACHEL: What did you mean earlier when you said that if you get the message from a pain you don't have to be sick?

ARNY: Let me give you an example. I just worked in another seminar with somebody who had previously been paralyzed for many years. She realized during meditative work that she was moving slightly forward from the hips. We started ampli-fying the movement by moving forward slowly, focusing on the movements. She suddenly felt again the experience of being paralyzed and froze.

The paralysis pattern came up in meditation and instead of leaving it, she stayed with it. She amplified the stiffness, paraly-sis and pain. She experienced the paralysis as her body pushing up against something. Focusing on that feeling, she switched channels and saw a picture of a piece of wood in her back that just wouldn't bend. "Stiff as a board," she said. She then began to move consciously like the stiff board and sat up like this. [*Arny sits up with a stiff back, looking surprisingly like a Zen master.*]

As she sat like this, she got to the real edge, and said to me, like a Zen master, stiffly, "This is my boundary. I am not adapting anymore to anyone!" Her paralysis was trying to get her to the point where she could manifest this definitiveness. She is an especially warm person who is capable of adapting, but her primary process of adapting is not completely congru-ent with her totality. She needs that piece of wood in the back, that paralysis, in order to be definitive, to set boundaries and to be less flexible with others. Integrating her earlier paralysis and stiffness was her meditation. After the work, the pain and stiff-ness were gone. Meditation can be helpful.

CHAPTER 5

Movement

A fter the morning work on meditation, the seminar continues with movement work. Arny explains how movement is a channel that works like a bridge between inner and outer experience.

Movement Theory

ARNY: Movement is a minority channel in psychology. There are many foolish prejudices against working with movement, which is probably why many dance therapists have inferiority feelings about their important work! The rest of the therapeutic world tends to treat people like stationary, analytical computers. When movement does turn up in therapy, it is often programmed rather than authentic.

Process work tries not to program movement; it discovers it. Weird, unexpected or ungraceful movements are not wrong, but are just what we're looking for! The unexpected movement is the one with the important message. Processing unintended movements helps us become unique individuals.

People talk a lot about individuality, I think, because they don't let it happen enough. The place where that is most obvious is in movement. Imagine how wonderful the world would be if people walked down the street and occasionally stopped and processed their spontaneous, unexpected, and unintentional movements. Then they would start hopping around like frogs, become T'ai Chi masters, fly like butterflies or grow immense and fat! Why not?

Movement work takes psychology out of private practice and makes it alive. It turns therapy into world theater. When we work with movement, psychology and therapy fade away, and instead ordinary reality becomes living art.

Amy is really the movement expert. She has studied it and has taught me a lot. Movement work relates very much to the world. It is also extremely easy to demonstrate and a very speedy access to secondary material.

But truly creative movement cannot occur without a differentiated meditative attitude which is able to pick up incomplete and disturbing movements. You cannot be spontaneous by just wanting to be. You need to develop awareness of unintentional experiences. Trying to move authentically without awareness or meditation is not quite satisfying, because without the awareness of edges or secondary movements, which I will show you in a moment, you just repeat your old standard, boring experiences. Truly authentic movement is unbelievable, shocking, and surprising.

You may have noticed in the last exercise how your spontaneous movement cannot be categorized as simply movement, for it is combined with vision, hearing, feeling, and relating and becomes an irreducible experience. Therefore, movement work, like dream and bodywork, does not really exist. Everything is awareness and process work. We need to train our awareness in all the various channels, realizing that they are the steps down to the river, not the water itself.

Movement Meditation

Now, let's bring our differentiated awareness to movement work and develop our meditation further. There are many ways to work with movement signals. Let's work with movement in two steps. Continuing with the meditative focus, we will start working internally with small movements. Later we will work with movement however it manifests itself.

In addition to focusing internally on seeing, hearing, and feeling, I would like you to focus your awareness on the movement which is spontaneously happening to you. Let me show you by first working on myself.

[*Arny rearranges his sitting position to get more comfortable. He sits erect and crosses one leg over the other. He continues to talk and simultaneously focuses on his inner experiences.*]

Let's say I'm in the middle of some kind of meditation experience and I'm following things inside of me. I'm seeing, hearing or feeling something, and at a certain moment I notice that I'm making very tiny movements by rocking my torso slightly on my pelvis.

My job is to notice and follow these very small movements. Because they are so slow and gentle they actually lie between proprioception and movement. [*Arny pauses as he speaks, his attention also focused on the subtle movements he is making.*]

I notice that I'm beginning to move even more. I'd like you to also move in such a way that you can discover how you move. What joints do you use? Which muscles move when you rotate in a sitting position? What does your skeleton do when stretching one leg? As I'm moving on my pelvis, I sense movements in the joints and muscles in my back.

After noticing these movements, amplify them, Don't just notice yourself moving, but move a little further, in slow motion, with greater awareness than before. Notice the mechanics of how you move, increase your spatial extension, decrease or increase your rhythm.

We make intentional and unintentional movements all the time. Just noticing an unintentional movement is already a big intervention. You can make immense discoveries about yourself by taking such unintentional movements to their edge.

[*Arny goes back to his movements. He moves forward very slowly on his pelvic axis.*] So I notice a little wiggle while sitting here in a sitting position. Now I'm going to take it to its edge. I'm going to allow this movement to continue to the maximum extension of my muscles, to the point where I can't move anymore. Completing a movement with this amount of awareness takes time. I sense myself moving down towards the floor, and feel my head going down all the way to the floor to pray! [*He pauses for a moment, staying in this position, then slowly sits up and begins to speak again.*]

I came across this type of work in Zurich, working with Barbara Croci, who was then a yoga teacher. It seems that hatha yoga could have developed from this form of movement meditation. Meditating on the smallest movements and amplifying them often leads to archetypal posturing which resembles what is now known as hatha yoga. By becoming aware of, amplifying, and following these small movements, you recreate yoga without necessarily having studied it.

During movement work you might find yourself crawling on your hands and knees, or working and meditating on all fours like a cat. This "cat" position, by the way, is a very valuable place to begin meditation since it gives you access to various back muscles.

Your body is unpredictable. The point is not to program yourself but to become aware of your movements when you

The cat

start to move. Bring movements to their edges, to the extremes, amplify them a bit. But please don't push yourself further than what feels right to you, because you can hurt yourself.

Find out how your muscles connect to your tendons and where your tendons connect with the bones. This is especially important for people interested in arthritic and rheumatic experiences.

Catch all your movements, even the weird, strange ones. Amplify them and use other tools too, like switching channels. At a certain point when the movement doesn't go further, switch channels and visualize the movement experience which is trying to happen. You could also use your hearing, of course, and listen for or make sounds which represent the movement.

If you find yourself getting up and suddenly you burp or feel pain, don't jump over these experiences. They are the crucial experiences asking for focus. If you ever manage by luck to come across a small pain, hold onto it. It is a magical treasure.

A participant asks Arny to explain what he means by "holding onto" a pain or an experience.

ARNY: Experiment and become aware of it. Feel it. How did that movement get created? Re-create it. If you find something happening, examine it. Whatever happens to you, do it, feel it, and see it more. Make sounds which represent it. Switch channels and make movements that go along with it. The idea is to explore and find out about it.

Don't throw away any little signal, movement, or pain. This work is a form of ecology. If you don't amplify and work with little pains, then they reappear in other areas of your body or in other channels, like relationship. You can't get rid of the information. You can only drive it away or ignore it temporarily. Making something out of almost nothing gives you a choice about becoming ill.

You can become ill by not paying attention to your proprioception. Meditation is a useful way to catch illnesses in their beginning stages. However, don't make a program out of the healing quality of awareness; it is not a panacea. Sometimes letting go of awareness is important too.

I am not certain that staying free of colds and sore throats is a good thing, but I haven't gotten one in fifteen years. I began this new phase of my life in a pretty weird way. In 1972, after having had a normal life of catching every kind of sickness, I made something like a warrior's decision to go up to the Swiss Alps and catch myself catching a cold.

I waited on a mountain in the canton of Glarus for a little breeze which would give me a chill. The breeze arrived! I felt it, and let my body move. I found myself running like hell behind an old oak tree to hide from the wind. I knew the wind was after me, and my body knew that it had to hide.

Thank God no one saw me doing that; they would have thought I was mad. I continued seeking breezes and running from them for several days. I developed a sense for the spirit behind colds and drafts, and have paid great respect to it ever since. I don't tell people what I am doing, but when I feel one of those little draft-spirits, I get out of its way, and then, if I feel strong enough, I get to know it better.

Exercise in Meditation

Now, I'd like to invite you to start working in a position that is generous to movement. For example, starting off in a yoga position like the cat position on all fours or a similar position opens you up to movement. Lying on the floor limits your movements to rolling around. You might want to start movement meditation from this position. [*Arny gets on all fours, with his elbows on the floor, and rests his head upon his two fists placed on top of one another on the floor. He stands up slowly and continues.*]

Do you know this position? My favorite meditation position is putting your back on the seat of a chair, letting your head drop down below the seat, and sticking your feet up in the air.

Beginning meditation

[*Changing position*] Sitting on your heels with your back straight is good for hip and pelvis movement. You can also start by sitting up against the wall and relaxing. Another good way to begin is by standing up very slowly. You could spend the whole day working with standing up. You could also begin from a standing position.

Now go ahead and work with your movement. Find out what channel you are in. Amplify the experiences you are having in that channel and follow the process as it winds through movement, seeing, hearing, and feeling. Then use a channel-changing technique and discover where your inner process wants you to be.

People begin the meditation. Most of the participants move slowly through various meditative postures. There is a feeling of intense

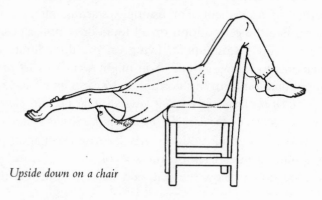

Upside down on a chair

concentration in the room. After about twenty minutes, Arny asks the people if they are finished or have any questions.

Questions

ARNY: An interesting question to ask in meditation is, "Who is meditating?" or "For whom are these experiences meant?" The experiences are not meant for just anybody and they don't come out of the clear blue sky. There is somebody in you who needs these particular experiences and isn't getting enough of them. There's a certain part of you that needs the particular experience, the message of your meditation. What you've just been experiencing is important for someone in you, for the one who is meditating. Finding out for whom the experience is meant increases the meaning of the meditation.

PAT (A shy young woman): I was sitting on this spot and I felt a burning in my crotch. I felt a pressure and sort of saw myself going down. Then I floated in and out of being aware of what was going on.

ARNY: The floating sounds like you reached an edge with experiencing the burning sensation. Stay with the burning for a while. You ought to check out what kind of sensation burning is.

PAT: What happened to me was that in the midst of my meditation, you came over and touched me to help amplify the movement I was making. Then my experience switched and I felt, "That's all I ever wanted. I just want someone to touch me."

ARNY: That sounds like the right message. You were working on opening up to relationship, to needs, touch, and contact. An interesting step further might be to meditate while holding someone's hand. I guess your burning crotch is a message for a part of you which tries to be alone.

Pat nods her head, indicating that she agrees with Arny's answer. Gary, another participant, seems troubled and starts to speak.

GARY: I got mental injunctions during my process. It seems to me there are different voices in there. Could you address that for a minute? What do you do about these little analytic comments?

ARNY: The archetypal voice is usually the interpreter in the background. He usually interprets and analyzes, saying what your experiences mean. Check him out and find out if he is good at what he is doing. Don't just repress him. Many inner critics are not as intelligent as they think they are. If you check them out, you will find that some might need to go back to school.

GARY: What do you mean, "Check him out"?

ARNY: Get more experience of the voice. What is the age and sex of the voice? Visualize a person that goes along with the voice. Interact with him or her. Make movements that go along with his or her image. Build an identity around it. Fill out the experience and then work with it.

I don't have any recipes. One of my inner critics used to be a great problem for me. I checked him out and discovered that he had a lot of opinions, but wasn't very smart. So I made him read books on symbols so he would know what he was talking about. After a while, he disappeared. I don't know what happened to him. I think he ran away from school!

AMY: In my experience, the commentator keeps coming back because I don't have enough information about him. It's useful to use movement and vision, to use other channels to get more background to the critic.

Working with Movement

Arny wants to continue talking about movement and the numerous ways one can amplify and work in this area. He turns to Amy, and asks her to talk about the ways of working with movement that she likes best.

AMY: We should mention special methods like forbidding or inhibiting signals and amplifying. Arny already spoke a bit about that. Obviously we have to mention mirroring the movement signals of a client so the client can see them. Also, it's fun to use your hands to sculpt movement, working with the movement which appears, and following the muscles and motions as they flow. This is a combination of body and movement work. And, of course, there is the movement work in which we just sit back and meditate on the mover.

ARNY: Let's show movement work now with someone who would like to work.

He asks the group if anyone would like to work with him. Sue volunteers. Arny assures her, "This is very simple. All we have to do is walk together." They begin walking around the inside of the circle in which the participants are sitting. It looks as if they are taking a leisurely stroll.

That's right. Let's just walk. While you are walking I'm going to ask you to notice if there is something inside your moving body which is not just walking.

[*As Sue is focusing on her movement, Arny talks to the group.*] You see, her primary process, which I'm setting up with her, *is* walking, but there may be something else which is unintentional that isn't just walking. [*To Sue*] Can you feel it or can you sense this other thing in your movements? Take your time. [*To the group*] Always keep your awareness open, not only to the things you are intending to do but also to the unintentional movements in life! [*To Sue*] So what is happening that is not just walking?

SUE: I'm aware of the group as I walk in the circle. I also feel something loose. Everything feels loose.

She moves her arms and legs loosely, showing Arny how loose she feels. He notices it and mirrors her with his arms.

ARNY: Go ahead, show me all the loose things!

Sue begins to exaggerate the looseness by swinging limbs, wobbling and wriggling around. She makes snake-like movements, and jumps from foot to foot. Arny follows her movements, making them with her. Her movement speeds up and she shakes her whole body from side to side like a rag doll. Suddenly, she seems to come to an edge. She stops and looks quickly at Arny. He encourages her to continue:

ARNY: Go on! Go ahead and take that to its extreme.

Beginning to move

Sue begins again, moving around the circle, shaking and swaying from side to side. Again she hesitates. Her movement changes from the loose swaying to that of an embarrassed child. She turns to Arny and says shyly, "Oops, I think I just hit an edge!" Everyone laughs.

Arny mimics the swaying motions she was making before, encouraging her to go back and pick them up again.

ARNY: Let's see where that movement would go if you were to take it right over the edge.

SUE: I became aware of this earlier today. One part of me really enjoys movement and there's another part of me which wants to keep me totally inert. There's a real polarity there, and a fight. [*As she speaks about the polarity she makes hand motions. One hand wriggles as she says she enjoys movement, and the other hand makes a "stop" motion when she describes being inert.*]

ARNY: OK, that is the edge. There is a fight and for the moment I'm going to go with the movement side since it hasn't been able to express itself completely. It's secondary. The inert side is primary and quiet. You know the quiet side already. [*He wiggles and entices her to move.*] You want to try again? I know this is embarrassing, but try it.

SUE: Let me walk a while so I'm not so aware of the group.

Her embarrassment to wriggle in front of the group indicates that the group now carries the projection of the movement inhibitor, the quiet side of her.

ARNY: The group stops you, right? I'm going to help you by making movements that are weird, too.

He stands across from her and wriggles. He swings his body and shakes his hips in a playful way. She instantly takes up the invitation and jumps sideways from one foot to the other, head and arms flopping with her torso. She raises her arms above her head, waves them like a hula dancer, and jumps faster and faster from one foot to the other. She makes indescribable, ecstatic motions, breaking free.

Arny encourages her to go all the way with movement. Sue suddenly flops, drops to the floor and, surprisingly, starts to tumble and roll. Finally, she pauses, out of breath, looks at Arny and exclaims with astonishment, "I didn't know I could do that!" The rest of the group cheers and claps for her.

ARNY: That was wild! That was wonderful. You didn't know you could do that, did you? You didn't know you could do what?
SUE: Those last little somersaults,
ARNY: Take a second and make a picture out of them.
SUE: That was me when I was six years old!
ARNY: Now if we were going to work with that little girl, the six-year-old, what sounds would she make?

Sue says she would giggle. With that, she starts to giggle and the group joins in. Arny, too, joins in the child's play and they laugh and giggle together. Arny moves closer to her and putting his arm around her shoulder, tries to read into her signals.

ARNY [*Adoringly*]: Nice little girl. She's looking for her mommy to take her shopping.
SUE [*Looks at him*]: I thought when you came over that my father never did that.
ARNY: Oh, the father. You need a mommy to take you shopping and a father, too, to support the child instead of inhibiting it.

Breaking free

Sue looks at Arny and suddenly understands that the father she mentioned is her inhibition against her movements.

SUE: Yeah. Thanks. Thank you.

Arny and Sue embrace, and Sue leaves the center of the circle. Everyone is quiet for a few minutes.

ARNY: Let's think together about what happened. Do you think that Sue somersaults in her everyday life?

TOM: She must. She does it so well!

ARNY: Yes, she must do it, but since her father, her primary identity—remember what she said, "I stop myself"—inhibits the six-year-old in her from wriggling around, her wriggling is secondary. It happens to her. She said she was surprised that she could do those flips and wriggles, so that means they are probably further from her awareness. They are split off from

The child

her ordinary identity because they are not "fathered" by her now. You see, we spontaneously remember parental images at a given moment, because they symbolize the way we care for the childlike parts of ourselves.

This kind of movement work takes awareness and a little tiny bit of courage. What was so interesting about her movement? It looked adult to me, but there was something in her movement that was not quite adult-like, something like a child.

Amy mimics the child's movements by shaking her arms in the air.

ARNY: See that. Those movements were less organized. They were not completing themselves. Therefore, they were secondary and the ones I went with. Remember, secondary movements do not complete themselves, they tend to repeat, they are difficult to understand and the person is usually embarrassed by or unconscious of them.

I can say this metaphorically: when she walks, she does not walk alone. When she walks, a little girl walks with her too. She walks together with a somersaulter, the happy one. When we walk, others walk with us as well. And the best job we could ever have is to find out who is walking with us!

Now, let's all try this movement work. Just start walking. You can work on yourself as you talk, sit or walk, with anything you do. The job is to simply catch the thing which is not doing what you are doing, and work with that.

Value the unexpected. The unexpected is the most valuable guide we have in this world. Notice the unexpected while walking. Feel the part which is not simply walking. And then experiment. Create art forms. Leave psychology and therapy behind. Let your movements become new forms of experience.

The group breaks up and starts walking around the room. After a few minutes the circle has transformed into something resembling a madhouse. One person is standing on her head, another is praying, others are making strange sounds and still another is hitting the wall. One woman is moving like a bird. A man walks like a hunchback, and some are just sitting quietly, working on themselves alone.

Arny and Amy move among the group, helping people amplify their movements. After about twenty minutes, some people begin to leave for lunch, while others remain involved in their inner experiences.

CHAPTER 6

Bodywork

A fter a lunch break, the seminar resumes in the early afternoon. Arny introduces the theme for the afternoon: bodywork.

ARNY: I'd like to talk about the kind of process work which begins with proprioception. This work is commonly called "bodywork." I am differentiating the normal concepts of bodywork from bodywork within the process work framework because the normal concept of the body usually focuses only on one channel. Our work can easily begin there, but usually moves outside the normal boundaries of the "body" and goes into other channels.

There are many forms of bodywork and many ways to access material and processes in the body. I think it would be fun to begin with the hands-on kind, because it is close to meditation, yet goes off into other, unpredictable events.

Example: Unfolding Chest Pressure

Instead of talking about it, I think it would be useful to do it with someone. Is there anybody who might like to work with me for a couple of minutes?

Ron volunteers. Ron and Arny stand up and move to the center of the circle. They sit down facing each other. Arny talks to Ron while simultaneously explaining to the group.

There are all sorts of ways to begin. We could start by talking, touching, shaking, vibrating, sensing without touching, or in any channel or any place which is right for the therapist and client. Instead of saying hello, I can also put a hand on you and find out about you that way. And you can answer physically as well.

Let me ask you a vague question which can be answered in many ways. If you were to allow me to put my hands on some part of your body, which part feels that it has the most process in it now?

Ron scans his body for a moment and then points to his chest.

ARNY: OK. How should I use my hands there? Would you like to lie down, or just sit where you are?

Ron says he'd like to lie down.

ARNY [*Nods*]: OK. Lie down. Your body is going to direct what happens.

Ron lies down and Arny sits next to him, by his chest. As he starts to work with Ron, he talks to the group.

I'm going to start by putting my hands on Ron's chest and I want you, from the outside, to watch when channels change. I'll be doing the same thing and then we'll talk about it afterwards. [*To Ron*] I'm going to use my hands on the top of your chest in several ways, and you tell me which one of them feels right. OK?

Ron nods.

Your body feelings will direct us.

Arny places his hands on Ron's chest and experiments with his fingertips and palms. He moves his hands in many different ways. First, he looks like he's massaging Ron's chest, and then he applies pressure, using his thumbs on specific points. Sometimes his hands seem to barely touch Ron's chest. After a few minutes of trying these different things, Arny uses his fingertips to explore specific areas of Ron's chest.

Now I'm going to put a more pointed pressure there. Go ahead and direct me about what sort of pressure and feelings you need.

Ron mumbles and sighs. He asks Arny to put more pressure higher on the chest. Arny readjusts what he's doing.

Good. I like your help. Is that right? Yeah?

Ron continues to direct Arny, asking him to apply more pressure and to push straight down.

Arny's hands are flat on the left side of Ron's chest. He moves them slowly toward the center. Ron takes a deep breath. Arny acknowledges this deep breath, thinking that Ron has entered into a proprioceptive process and the breath is good feedback. Ron's inhalation exerts pressure against Arny's hands; it is an attempt to feel more, which is positive feedback. Negative feedback to the pressure would be a lack of reaction or a movement away from the pressure.

RON: Mmm, please move your right hand more towards my throat. More pressure with your left hand.

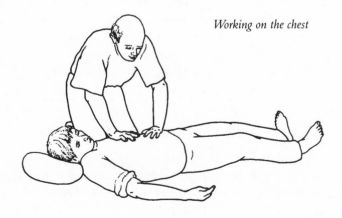

Working on the chest

Arny moves his right hand toward the throat and applies still more pressure with the left hand on the top of Ron's chest. Ron sighs again, more deeply.

ARNY: Is that the right amount of pressure? Less? More?

Ron closes his eyes and tells Arny he feels more relaxed. Arny grunts in agreement. Ron takes another deep breath.

ARNY: I like the big breath.

RON: It seems like your pressure is counteractive to some internal pain I have.

ARNY: I am countering something in there. OK. Let me feel it from inside. The encountering.

Ron pushes up with his chest against Arny's hands. With his jaw open and eyes closed, Ron tries a number of times to push his chest against Arny's pressure. Ron takes a deep breath and exhales loudly.

Yeah, that is a big breath. Go ahead and take it.

Ron breathes and his arms drop from his abdomen to the floor. He breathes deeply in and out. Arny turns to the group while still working with Ron and talks softly to them.

So I am encountering an experience under there, a movement and pressure against mine, and that itself is the beginning or perhaps the end of the work. The rest is now processing the encounter. Some of you might even be able to imagine what the counter-pressure in the chest is about, especially if you have some experience with breathing.

[*To Ron*] I am going to take my hands off for a moment and see if you can still feel the encounter. [*Arny very slowly takes his hands away.*]

RON: I feel a pressure in my chest and a slight choking in my throat. And a queasiness...

Arny returns to the encounter by applying more pressure. He puts one hand on the rib cage, the other near Ron's throat.

RON: Yeah, maybe even a little harder.

Arny is surprised by how much pressure Ron requests. He almost has his full weight on Ron and still Ron asks for more pressure.

RON: As soon as you press, I feel a sense of relief and I expand. [*He exhales deeply.*]

ARNY [*To Ron as he lies there with his eyes closed*]: Yes, so I am taking over something that is happening in your chest. [*Arny attempts to change channels.*] I'm going to do it even more. I am going to use my vocal cords and make sounds that go along with this pressure.

Arny starts to grunt, groan, growl, and make an assortment of different noises. Ron begins to respond almost immediately with sounds, and growls, "Aaaahhhh...ahhhh."

Arny is now facing Ron from above, with his hands still on the center of his chest, one on top of the other. Ron begins to cough. Arny guesses that the cough may be a reaction against the pressure. Acting a bit provocatively, Arny says, "Mhmm, trying to cough, are you?"

Ron opens his mouth widely and roars at Arny.

ARNY: You're not supposed to make noises! [*He switches back to his normal identity and whispers to Ron.*] Go ahead!

RON: Did you say I am or I'm not?

Arny realizes that Ron did not understand that the intervention was meant to be provocative. Ron used the vagueness of the intervention to assume that Arny was recommending something to him.

ARNY: Whichever you heard will be right. What did you hear?

RON: That I'm supposed to make noise.

Arny drops his intended intervention of challenging Ron and decides to follow him.

ARNY: Right, you are. You're supposed to make noises!

Ron exhales deeply and makes sounds. He then stops and complains that he is blocked and can't go further.

RON: I definitely don't want to know about those sounds. I'm starting to get confused. I touch it and then, whew, it's gone.

Arny assumes that Ron is at an edge and decides to follow Ron's avoidance and leave the whole thing behind.

ARNY: Yeah, let's jump away from it.
RON: I'm feeling dizzy.

Arny assumes that all the confusion and mixed responses are indicative of the edge, which forbids further exploration.

ARNY [*In a light and humorous tone*]: I'll just put some pressure on the top of you and we can talk about the weather. Nice weather today?
RON [*Laughs*]: Great. It's a sunny day. Beautiful.
ARNY [*Takes his hands off Ron and sits back*]: It's a sunny day. A great day for doing process work here.

Ron looks relieved and says he feels much better. He pauses, and then speaks to Arny.

RON: I'm worried you're going to come back to my chest.
ARNY [*Ignores this comment*]: Well, the weather is not bad. It's a little cooler, thank God, and the fog is moving down the coast. You know, the last time I was here there was no sun.
RON [*Suspiciously*]: I don't trust your discussion of the weather.
ARNY [*Looks at him mischievously and teases him*]: You don't trust my discussion of the weather?

The rest of the group starts to laugh.

I think you are very wise!
RON: I think I've been here before. Not with you, but with other therapists. There's lots of stuff going on inside of me.
ARNY [*Continues to be lighthearted*]: Well, don't pay attention to it.

The group laughs.

Yes, humor. Well, let's get back to the coastal weather.
RON [*Begins to look a bit nervous*]: I'm not sure why I'm getting more and more anxious. I have a suspicion. [*He takes a big breath.*]

ARNY: You have a hunch? That was a big breath. Edges are important to have. [*Arny leans over and puts one hand back on Ron's chest.*] Should we go back there?

Ron nods, yes.

You tell me when you are ready.

Arny is hoping for a shortcut to access the secondary process. He sees that Ron's more primary state or everyday experience is to be the victim of a pressure in his chest. Arny's goal at this point is to switch the roles and give Ron access to his secondary process, the one making the pressure. He wants to find out what information or what kind of state is located in the pressure-maker.

Maybe it would even be easier for you to show me the kind of pressure that you have on your chest by doing it to me. Want to try that? I'm going to lie down, and you show me the pressure that you have.

Ron gets up immediately. The speed with which he takes up Arny's suggestion is positive feedback, that is, it gives Arny the idea that his suggestion is on the right track. Arny lies down. Ron crawls over to Arny's side and puts his right hand on top of Arny's chest and his left hand lower down on the chest and applies pressure.

ARNY [*Encourages Ron*]: Yeah, that's it. That's really good. Hold that for a minute. I'm going to make little tiny resistance

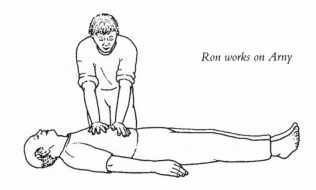

Ron works on Arny

movements. You do what you're doing and I'm going to do what I'm doing. OK? [*Ron nods. Arny simultaneously resists the pressure and talks to Ron, who is above him pressing on his chest.*] Now, let's say my name is Ron and you can be anyone you want up there.

[*Playing Ron*] What have you got against me? You're not letting me up.

Arny is practicing a form of dual awareness. He is playing two parts at once: the resister (Ron's normal, primary self) and the therapist helping Ron to be the pressure-maker. The way he is talking to Ron is very important. He uses one tone to play the resister, and another to help Ron be the pressure-maker. He switches back and forth, not just playing a role, but simultaneously keeping his awareness on Ron, watching for feedback, and helping him get into another part.

ARNY [*Whispering loudly to Ron*]: Go ahead and do what you're doing as long as you can. [*Arny switches to the resister role.*] I'm not a bad guy, why are you putting this pressure on me all the time? [*Arny gives Ron resistance to help him feel the pressure he is applying. Arny wriggles around underneath Ron, trying to get away, and then starts talking to Ron, the pressure-maker, imagining intuitively into Ron's past.*]

You damn pressure-maker! I tried to massage you out twenty times already. But you're still here, damn! Uhgh!! What do you do when you have something like this on top of you?

Ron is now using his strength and makes a determined face. Arny notices it and, trying to help Ron more into the role of pressure-maker, comments on it.

I like your face!

RON [*Looks excited*]: This one up here, the pressure-maker, is quite interesting!

ARNY [*As the resister*]: I'm going to get rid of you once and for all! One, two, three, four, five, and... [*He pushes against Ron's arms.*] Damn you! You've been around much too long. I gotta get this thing off of me. I've tried to massage you away but that doesn't work.

Arny pushes harder while encouraging Ron to maintain his pressure. A real battle ensues. While they're struggling physically Arny sees that he's accessed Ron's strong side and wants to keep the part around long enough to discover why it is here. The method he chooses to do this is switching channels, putting the experience that's now in feeling and movement into talking.

ARNY: OK. I'm going to let you do your job, but listen here, demon, this time when you do it I want you to know why you are doing it.

RON [*Fights back, yelling*]: I won't let you go!

Arny tries to fight his way up, but Ron tries to keep him down, pressing on his chest.

RON: Get down. Don't ever get up. You're under my control. You don't have any right to get up. I have all the power.

ARNY [*Goes down to his knees*]: I'm sorry. I sometimes have a mind of my own. You've had all the power around here. Tell me more about yourself.

RON: I actually have a hold of you inside. It's like I'm clamping your chest. I'm holding you down, and I don't want to tell you who I am.

Arny suddenly stops talking as if he were in an opposing role, and identifies Ron with this new behavior.

ARNY: This is the part of you I want to know. [*He grabs Ron.*] This is the strong side I was hoping to bring out.

RON [*Pauses thoughtfully*]: I am determined.

ARNY: Tell me some of the things you are determined to do.

RON [*Looking meanly at Arny*]: First thing is to keep you under control. That's taken care of. And you definitely can't feel at ease. Definitely don't like yourself, your looks, size. You are weak and old. You're impotent, sick, puny, small. You're going to get sick.

ARNY: Yeah? Well, you're pretty nasty. You're the nastiest thing I've seen in days. I like it. I want you to be more like that.

*Ron and Arny
locked in combat*

Ron stands up straight and looks down at Arny. He's about a foot taller than Arny. Their arms are still locked in combat, and they continue struggling with each other.

ARNY: Go ahead and really be nasty now. Can you demand something more from me?

RON: I'm having a hard time with you because you're not under control. Whew, I'm off.

ARNY: You're off, aren't you? So this is the organic moment to switch roles.

Arny now plays the nasty powerful one, but this time with all the information he got from the foregoing process.

ARNY [*Loudly*]: I want you to follow me! You have to do everything I tell you to do. Get down!

Ron goes down on his knees.

Hate yourself! You're a good-for-nothing puny son of a bitch. When I tell you to do something in the future, I want you to do it! I control the show around here.

RON [*Hesitates and then stands up*]: It's interesting. My first instinct is to follow the instructions.

Arny continues in the nasty role.

ARNY: Well, follow them! What are you standing up for? Who do you think you are around here? Get down. You are supposed to get down! For Godsakes, you're breaking up the pattern.

Ron starts to shake his hands, as if to warn Arny, and then he stops. Apparently he is at an edge. To help him over this impasse, Arny challenges him even more.

> Don't shake your hands. Get down and follow me when I tell you what to do. You puny weakling!

RON [*Approaches Arny, grabs his arms threateningly and yells*]: No!

ARNY [*Emphatically*]: Yes! When I press your chest, it's supposed to collapse. You are not supposed to come out and do anything against me. This is not right. I want you to follow orders now. Down!

> [*Arny puts his hands on Ron's shoulders and they fight. Arny continues to provoke Ron.*] I told you to get down and I meant it. Goddammit! Get the hell down! DOWN! I'm telling you to go down. Since when have you disobeyed me? You're supposed to be a nothing.

Ron glares at him and starts to push him menacingly and powerfully. He quickly darts behind Arny, picks him up and puts him outside of the circle. While being lifted into the air, Arny yells exuberantly, "That's it, great!!"

RON: I just have to pick you up. It's amazing how much I've been listening to you.

Everyone laughs. One of the participants yells that Ron should listen to Arny. Ron responds by taking over. He goes to Arny, picks him up again and drops him on top of the participant.

RON: Huh! I get it! This is the same energy that the evil pressure-maker had, except that it has a different use. If I could be strong enough, I would just put you on a shelf!

Arny is now standing again on his own two feet. There is great relief in the room.

ARNY: Yeah, you get him out of your chest by using his energy.

RON [*Suddenly has an insight*]: Yeah. In other work I've done on this, we tried to remove the pressure. And so I guess I was inadvertently provoking the pressure-maker, increasing it, feeding the fire.

ARNY: Instead of using it.

RON: Yeah. That's it. You've got the right idea.

Arny makes a growling noise and mirrors Ron's powerful part to show him his power, and Ron growls back. Arny goes over to Ron and they embrace. Ron thanks Arny and they both sit down. Arny looks around and talks to the group.

ARNY: What did you see? Ron has done other work on that to get rid of the pressure. Why was it difficult for Ron to get in touch with that particular energy under there?

ERIC: It's an edge.

ARNY: Yes. He wanted to remove it, not use it. That pressure-maker is an identity crisis. For him to get in contact with that critical energy he'll have to get in contact with this [*He makes a fist*], like he did in the beginning. He'll have to be able to go up to someone and feel or say [*Pointing to the ground*], "When I say something I want you to do it."

Ron takes over

Why do you think he took a deep breath when I put my hand on his chest? He was relieved! Isn't that fascinating? When you have a headache or pressure, if somebody makes more pressure, it is relieving. The same holds true in your body. If you make a pressure similar to that which is happening to you, it's relieving. You experience relief from the deeper internal cramp, because the cramp relaxes as soon as it is countered by a similar energy. Something powerful like a cramp relaxes as soon as you, too, become powerful and take a stand against it. Ron's deep inhaling breath is a countering reaction. His breath was the beginning of the opponent of the critical pressure-maker. The great breath is the beginning of a fight.

Parts Versus Process

In every breath there is the primary experience of trying to get room, and the secondary experience is the thing taking the room away. When you breathe, you are breathing against something, creating space or making room because there is some other feeling of not having enough room. So the primary experience, the one you are doing, is breathing, making more room. The secondary part, the one happening to you, is the thing which is taking away your room, the cramp itself.

As always, it is this damn secondary experience which is asking to be met energetically and physically integrated. The element furthest from awareness is the critical figure behind the cramp. But we cannot just throw out the critic or the cramp or the evil one. We need to use its intense energy. The thing which seems to be the enemy is almost always the greatest ally! We don't need its thoughts or what it has to say, but we need its energy.

In every body experience there are at least two parts. Even an itch has a scratcher and the one irritating the scratcher. One part is closer to our identity and the other is farther away. We need to remember that, even though the client experiences one part as being good and the other as being bad, we must side with the whole, not with any one part.

Many of you will be tempted to feel the way the client feels, and will want to take sides with the primary process. Standing for the wholeness and individuation of the client, however, means standing for the entire process and not for the parts. The task of the therapist is to give the whole process, both parts, a chance to express themselves.

Once you start to work with the parts, they begin to be more flexible as they exchange information with one another. Before you know it, good and bad, strong and weak, old and young disappear. There is no longer yin or yang, there is only the Tao, the process itself, the flow of energy which we focus on.

This is what happened with Ron. In the beginning there was just a cramp. Then there were two parts: the critic and its victim. Finally, both parts melted together. He overcame the cramper by taking over its energy. In so doing he resembled the cramper and both parts became one. Neither part was good or bad. In the end we were left with the powerful, definitive energy which is Ron's true process in the moment.

Notes on Working

When you work with one another, remember that when you put your hand on someone and relieve them of a pressure, you are accessing a secondary process. Wait until they're ready to pick up what you're doing. You can't just tell them to switch roles.

Be careful when you work. Do not interpret your client's signals, but give the signals room to unravel themselves. For example, you may think that a facial expression looks like anger or surprise, but go back to sensory-grounded information. Look at the face. Describe the eyes, the cheekbones, the mouth. Ask, touch, guess, but do not interpret or act as if you know.

When you work, have a good time, but keep your eyes open and your ears clean, and be aware of both your own and the other person's movements. Follow the process. Notice when a role is finished. Only when the person really finishes with a role is it the organic moment to leave it and switch. When you can no longer play a role, then the person you are working with has annihilated the figure, integrated it or become it.

I'd like you to start by asking this vague question. [*He turns to the woman next to him.*] For example, let's say the two of us work together. Do you know what part of your body has the most process in it?

The woman immediately points to her feet and the bottom of her heels.

ARNY [*To the group*]: Everyone knows where their process is happening. They will tell you or their bodies will show you how to work. The body always works on the right place. It's wonderful.

Next, put your hand on your client where she directs you to. Follow her instructions about the amount of pressure, which part of the hand to use and where to go. Then follow the channel changes. Remember Ron? First he was feeling proprioceptively in his chest. Then came the movement in his chest, which we noticed first through his breathing. We followed that movement and it went into his arms. Then came sounds, or auditory experience. Then there was dialogue and movement, and, finally, he had an image of putting me on the shelf.

Follow how the channels and roles change and let the process unfold. Don't think you have to succeed at the whole thing. This is a training exercise for you to develop your awareness in following people as they go through dreamland.

At a given point, your client will step into the secondary process that has been disturbing her and then the dark mysterious side of the personality is in the light. She is then on the verge of experiencing her wholeness. This experience is the greatest goal. Neither one part nor the other is the answer. The interaction, awareness and experience of both parts is our goal.

Don't strive for relaxation or any other physical state, because the body can only relax when the experiences and messages in it are appreciated. Relaxation can even be dangerous because if you relax the body, the information in the tension may have to travel to a less tractable area, an area that is more difficult to reach.

AMY: I just wanted to mention how you were sitting with Ron. You sat like a lever so that you didn't exhaust yourself while you were working. I think that is important.

ARNY: Absolutely. Work in the way that is mechanically and physically the best for you, regardless of what you are doing, whether you are reading, writing or even if you are wrestling. I want you to think about your own body at all times, especially as a therapist. If you reach an edge inside of yourself and feel what you are doing is not right for you, don't do it.

HENRY: Let's assume you are working with somebody who is not into psychology and does not understand process. What other words could you use instead of "Where is the process in your body?"

ARNY: That's a good question. I'm into life, not psychology. And I must admit that I also don't really know what "process" means! Therefore, it's the best term. You can say anything that is vague, like, "Tell me where the thing is in your body that I should put my hand on?" or "Where do you feel something happening in your body?" Be honest. If people say "What do you mean?" you have to admit, "I don't know."

You see, vagueness is the point. Blankness is openness and therefore accesses the secondary material. It frees people to create and project into what you are saying. The idea of blankness is similar to the idea of the Rorschach test, which allows you to see your dreams. Nourish your vagueness and protect mysteriousness. They are our most powerful tools. The more vague you are, the more creative and free others feel. Start with the question, "Where do you feel process in your body now?"

CHAPTER 7

Chronic Symptoms

The participants work in pairs using the hands-on techniques that Arny demonstrated while Arny Amy walk around the room and help those who feel stuck. When the exercise is over, Arny asks the participants how it went. Mike complains that he got stuck in the bodywork. He touches the back of his right shoulder and shows Arny what they were working on. "I felt stuck in moving," he says.

ARNY: I saw you make a hand motion. I'm glad you did that because it is something I wanted to discuss. [*To the others*] Did you see Mike do this just now? Watch me. People describe things much better with their hands than they do verbally.

[*Arny imitates Mike's hand motion and then asks the participants if they noticed it. He then turns to Mike.*] Can you also say what was back there?

MIKE: It's still there. It's tension that is blocked. It's knotted. [*He makes another gesture with his hand as he describes the feeling in his shoulder. His hand makes a fist.*]

ARNY [*Sees the fist*]: Would you make that knot with your hand again?

Mike clenches his fist and shows it to Arny.

Right shoulder trouble

So, that's what you're stuck with. Makes a lot of sense to me. Take a look at it. Use your eyes now. What does it look like?

MIKE [*Instead of looking, says impatiently to Arny*]: We talked about it so much already. I tend to intellectualize about it.

ARNY: Well, instead of being stuck, tell me your first intellectualization of what you see.
MIKE: Thinking about being blocked and stuck.
ARNY: Hmmm. It's an edge to see something. In other words, when you look at it with your eyes you don't see anything?
MIKE: If I look at the hand?
ARNY: Yes. What do you see?
MIKE: My hand.
ARNY: You see a hand. Does your hand look like this? [*Arny makes an open hand.*]
MIKE: No.

Arny is using misinterpretation as an intervention. He deliberately makes statements and shows types of hands that must be corrected. Next he makes a claw and shows it to Mike.

ARNY: Does it look like this?
MIKE [*Shakes his head*]: No. It looks like a fist.
ARNY [*Smiling*]: Like a fist. That's very right.

Mike looks alternately down at his hand and then up to Arny.

ARNY: Let's just pretend that the other hand was going to make a fist too. Let's try that.

Mike makes fists with both hands.

Let's pretend that those fists are there for a good reason. Don't feel it or see it, just make up a reason why those fists are there. Just make it up.

MIKE [*Looks perplexed*]: Well...

ARNY [*Prompts him*]: Give me a reason why people make fists like that.

[*As Arny asks Mike this question, he holds his own fists out in front of him. He comically exaggerates the fists and the stance and Mike starts to laugh. Arny turns to the group.*] This is what you call an edge. Edges are truly a part of our elusiveness. We'll see more of that in a minute. [*Looking back at Mike, he tries again to get a response.*] Why do people normally make fists?

Mike stands with his arms straight out in front of him, with two fists clenched. He looks up at Arny.

MIKE: To punch things!

ARNY [*Looks amused*]: To punch things, yes. And what sort of *things* do people punch when they make fists?

MIKE: You mean what kind of *people* do you punch?

ARNY: That's right! What kind of *people?*

There is a ripple of laughter in the group. Mike thinks for a moment.

I guess you punch people who you want to punch! [*He makes a very hesitant punching motion with his right arm.*]

ARNY: That makes a lot of sense. I saw you make a slight movement with your right arm when you said that.

MIKE: This is my punching arm.

The movement in his arm indicates to Arny that there is a channel switch from visualizing and fantasizing to moving and punching. Arny makes an intervention that uses both the visual and kinesthetic channels.

ARNY: Your punching arm, hmm. Why don't you go through a slow-motion movement? Go ahead and punch, and see if you can imagine somebody that you would like to punch.

Mike draws his right arm back in a slow-motion punch. As he comes forward with his punch, he pauses and turns to Arny.

MIKE: For some reason I thought of an old neighbor of mine, Jim.

ARNY: Do you want to say something about him? What didn't you like about him?

MIKE: Well, we made nicknames up for him in the neighborhood. He lied.

ARNY: About what?

MIKE: He talked about me and lied behind my back. He said some nasty things.

Arny thinks that there might be a connection between the neighbor talking about Mike behind his back and the tension in his back.

ARNY: What did he say about you behind your back?

MIKE: I don't even know anymore.

ARNY: Tell me what you don't want to know anymore. Take a guess.

MIKE [*Looks lost in thought*]: I don't know. It's blank.

ARNY: That's a good thing to be blank about. Amnesia, forgetfulness. Let's see if you can fill the blank in with some thoughts of Jim's. [*To the group*] What do you think Jim thought behind Mike's back? [*To Mike*] Do you think he said you were a wonderful, fantastic guy?

MIKE [*Shakes his head*]: No.

ARNY: I don't think so either. What do you think he said?

MIKE: He said something I guess I didn't like. I remember feeling really betrayed.

ARNY: Behind your back he, I mean you, say negative things about yourself and this makes you angry back there. By the way, *behind your back* is where your problem is.

MIKE [*Nods yes, but doesn't look convinced; says sadly*]: I wish I could understand it.

ARNY [*Laughing*]: Well, don't. Just forget it. It's a real edge to support yourself. It's much easier to talk behind your back against yourself.

MIKE: What do I do with all that negativity?

Questions are always followed by somatic answers. Arny watches Mike to see how he answers his own question somatically. Mike unconsciously opens and closes his hand and then looks at it.

ARNY: He's showing us that when he comes to an edge to react against his own inner negativity, the reactions go into his fist and into his back.

MIKE: I don't know. The fist isn't tight. It's not like a fist anymore. Somehow I don't think it is Jim.

ARNY: No. I don't think it's Jim either. I think I know who it is. Do you know who it is?

MIKE [*Suddenly brightens*]: It must be me! I am angry at myself for being nasty to myself!

Edges and Negative Feedback

Arny and Mike sit down after a few minutes of talking. Arny turns back to the group and talks to them.

ARNY: That was a good example of an edge. When someone's at an edge, one part of the person says, "Help," and another part says, "I don't need help. I don't want to know what could happen."

Sometimes edges and negative feedback can be confused. The difference between negative feedback and an edge is that the edge has more energy. The person is truly split; one part wants to go into the new territory, but the other part is a bit frightened. At the edge we get confused, distracted, nervous, and jumpy.

When you're on the wrong track with a person, the client doesn't only avoid the intervention, but also implies something like, "What you are asking is not where I sense things must go." Here Mike was clearly at an edge. He said, "Yes, help," but then, "No, it is too much to be angry at my own negativity, though I do want to have my reactions."

Chronic Symptoms and Childhood Dreams

How many of you know about the connections between chronic symptoms and childhood dreams?

A few people raise their hands, but most haven't heard this concept.

Well, Jung discovered that childhood dreams are like personal myths; they determine long-term life patterns. I experimented with childhood dreams and found out that they also mirrored chronic symptoms.

You can guess the chronic body symptoms people have from their earliest dreams or memories. Both early or first childhood memories and childhood dreams tell the same story. You can use both as descriptions of the patterns of your life.

Let me tell you about a client Amy, Nisha, and I worked with recently. I will tell you his childhood dream and you tell me his symptoms. His earliest childhood memory is that he is sitting and playing in the corner of a sunny room. That's his first childhood memory, sitting in a room relaxing as the warm sun shines in. Isn't that a beautiful dream? Can you imagine a chronic symptom that would go along with that?

People make various guesses. Someone says that it would be a symptom like heartburn, while someone else mentions perspiration.

ARNY: Remember, he described the situation in his childhood dream as being very relaxing.

One participant suggests it could be exhaustion.

You're getting closer.

Someone else says it might be passivity.

You've almost got it. Imagine a symptom that would mirror extreme relaxation and passivity.

A woman remarks that it could be multiple sclerosis.

That's close enough. This man has ALS disease. His muscles are deteriorating and he cannot move or live without a respirator.

Childhood dreams try to become real. One of the funny ways they do this is by organizing your body symptoms. Some symptoms are so close to your identity that you might forget about them. Others are connected with secondary processes, with faraway identities, and can be very frightening.

For example, [*He takes off his glasses*] if you ask me how I am physically, I probably wouldn't mention my nearsightedness, the fact that I don't see well at great distances, because that problem belongs to my present identity. Nearsightedness does not disturb me much. I identify with it. I actually identify with being deep inside myself, which is how I experience being nearsighted. Symptoms connected to the primary process are not experienced as disturbing, whereas symptoms connected to the secondary process, those which disturb us and with which we do not identify, are usually very scary.

Whether something is a symptom or not depends upon your primary process and the kind of culture that you live in. For instance, for some people, low blood pressure might be a symptom of their primary process. Such people would identify with the weakness and fatigue which go along with low blood pressure and thus no longer experience it as a disturbance.

Secondary process symptoms are always more terrifying. They are the ones connected to the most powerful figures in your childhood dreams. The man with the dream of the sun is very introverted and shy. His secondary process is the sun itself, beaming outward, warming him and others. Thus, that extroverted warmth of the sun is secondary, but in the moment he is its "victim." It not only warms him up, but also creates complete relaxation, or paralysis.

Think about another dream figure, such as a tiger. [*He makes claws with his hands.*] Imagine a dream where a tiger wants to eat everything up in a bakery. What kind of chronic symptoms would go along with a tiger in a bakery in a childhood dream?

LINDA: Scratching, maybe psoriasis?

ARNY: Psoriasis could do it. The tiger woman has violent itchy eczema. [*He roars like a tiger and makes clawing motions.*] It's the tiger in her, trying to say hello. She wants to be sweet, but her secondary process is the tiger.

Working with Deafness

ARNY: I'd like to work with someone now on a chronic symptom and a childhood dream. Would somebody like to do that?

A number of people raise their hands. A man sitting in the group calls out that Kathy, another participant, should work. Arny turns to the man.

ARNY: Are you pointing to Kathy? Why?
TOM: I wanted to make sure that she worked.

The group laughs, and Arny asks the rest of the group what he should do. Members of the group shout that he should spin a pen. Arny gives the pen a spin and it lands, sure enough, on Kathy! Arny and the group are very surprised.

ARNY: Kathy, do you have a chronic symptom?
KATHY: I have a chronic ear syndrome [*She points to her ear and moves her hands around*] with vertigo and deafness in one ear. They think it's an auto-immune thing, but they're not sure what it is. Maybe I have an auto-immune problem.
ARNY: They don't know the cause, so they guess it is an auto-immune thing. But the symptom itself is deafness and dizziness?
KATHY: The dizziness is no more, but there used to be severe vertigo effects.
ARNY: Before we get deeper into it, did you have a recurring dream when you were a child?
KATHY: I actually did. It's not a dream, but it nonetheless comes to mind. I had this memory of a ritual, of light shining through a window. [*She raises her hands above her head and moves her fingers.*] I had a whole ritual of making many shadow figures every night.

This is also something which would wake me up. It was actually a terrifying event. It happened a lot. I suddenly realized that I was not going to live forever. I would get this feeling when coming out of this dream. I would go to the bathroom and call my sister.

ARNY: Realizing you were not going to live forever?

KATHY: Yeah, that's right. The feeling that came was like reaching up [*She puts her arms up again towards the sky.*] and waiting for my parents to save me. Just reaching. Most of my dreams are very happy, but that one was... very scary.

Arny nods, empathizing with her. Arny recommends that she follow her desire to work on the symptom, believing that the dream will be explained through working on the deafness. She agrees. They both move to the middle of the room and sit across from each other.

ARNY: How do you know that you are deaf?

KATHY [*Points to ear*]: I am deaf in my left ear. Actually I can hear a little bit.

ARNY: How much? This much? [*He mimics the gesture she had made earlier.*]

KATHY: No, this much. [*She holds her hands about a foot apart.*] I absolutely know because I cannot talk on the phone with my left ear. (*She puts her hand up to her ear as on the phone.*) And if I am listening to people I get tense, because I can't hear them. [*She looks down a bit and her voice quivers.*]

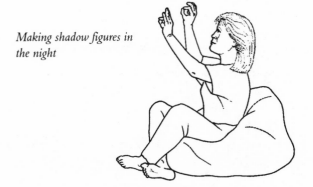

Making shadow figures in the night

ARNY [*To the others*]: How can we work with that symptom? How do your hearts and minds work? By pointing to her ear, she shows me that her symptom is experienced in the moment as an auditory signal or disturbance. [*To Kathy*] So what I am going to do is to sit on the left side of you, and talk to you in this ear in such a way that you can hear me. Your job is to trace the experiences that happen to you as my voice begins to get weaker. Do you want to try that?

Kathy nods.

> So I am talking now. Hello, this is Arny in Zurich. Are you there?
>
> [*Arny waits to hear a response.*] Oh, the telephone lines are not as good as they used to be. It must be the transcontinental connection. [*Arny continuously lowers his voice as he talks. He's almost whispering now.*] The connection is not as loud as it used to be. But we still have some auditory contact. What experiences do you have when my voice goes down?

KATHY [*Looks scared*]: A feeling of panic in my chest.

ARNY [*Decides to amplify this*]: Go ahead and follow the panic in your chest, as I move away, and see if you can give it more expression.

Kathy takes a big breath, and then begins to cry.

ARNY [*Very quietly*]: Can you still hear me?

KATHY: I feel I will be left behind and lost.

ARNY: Lost?

Role playing: on the phone

KATHY: Oh! My hearing suddenly got better. I can hear!

Arny hypothesizes that the symptom disappears when she feels her loneliness. Perhaps this feeling was the goal of the symptom. He talks to her in a very quiet voice, still "on the line" with her.

ARNY: How interesting. The connection is getting poorer, but when you feel panic, your hearing improves!

KATHY: Right now I do not know what you are talking to me about. And that really scares me. [*She sniffs and blows her nose.*]

ARNY [*Moving still further away*]: I am still here. I cannot speak louder. Even at this distance from you I am still fascinated by your panic. [*Now in a louder voice*] Could you show me the panic?

KATHY [*Starts to speak*]: My heart feels... [*She falls silent. She moves her hands expressively and then beats on her chest with her hands.*]

ARNY [*Encourages her to continue the motions*]: Do that, go ahead.

KATHY [*Looks a bit shy and laughs*]: It's exhausting. [*She stops, shivers a bit, looks down and drops her hands to her sides.*]

ARNY: That is what we call an edge! It's probably too much for you. OK. Why don't you just withdraw into your own world?

KATHY [*Shakes her head and says very softly*]: I can't do it.

ARNY [*Slowly moves further away from her and whispers*]: Bye-bye.

Kathy puts her head in her hand and sobs.

KATHY: All I hear is your voice, not what you are saying.

ARNY: My voice is saying that something is separating us for some unknown reason.

Kathy holds her head and cries. At this point, she doesn't hear or relate to Arny at all, but just looks down and sobs. Arny stops moving back and comes a bit closer. He looks sad.

ARNY [*Softly*]: I'm sorry it is so painful. I hate this too, but there may be something in it which will be good after all. Are you there?

Kathy doesn't answer, but continues to cry.

It's painful for me, too. I'm withdrawing. Are you there on the other side?

Kathy gestures helplessly.

> [*Arny raises his voice.*] I'll give you a hint. At this distance, the key you have, and probably the only key you will ever have, is to believe in the experiences inside of you and let them unfold. That is the crazy key.

Kathy nods in understanding.

> That key will bring this to the right conclusion. Even though my voice is now getting quieter and withdrawing, believe the experiences inside of you, and encourage them to happen.
>
> [*Arny turns to the group.*] From the outside you may already know something about her difficulty with hearing. How can we tell just by looking at her sitting quietly, occasionally shaking, what is primary and secondary at this point?

Arny thinks to himself that her normal primary identity is to be shy and withdrawn, and the experiences that are happening to her · in the shaking and vibrating could perhaps be to reach out and go after people. He moves even farther away.

ARNY: Follow your experiences now. I am withdrawing.

KATHY: I have a lot of tears. I am not sure I should be working. [*She looks at Arny and laughs.*]

ARNY: Amy, could you take over my job? Get on the telephone and speak to her, and I will be her aid in California and help her with her position.

Arny comes over to Kathy and Amy takes his position across the room. Arny sits next to Kathy and talks to her.

> While Amy is withdrawing, you can hear me pretty well now, can't you?

Kathy nods.

> [*Arny gets on the phone to Amy, and says loudly*] Amy, are you over there on the other side of the line?

AMY: Yes, I'm here in Zurich.

ARNY [*Turns to Kathy*]: Can we still hear Amy?

KATHY [*Shakes her head*]: No. I hear her voice, but not words. I don't hear what she says.

AMY [*Quietly*]: Kathy, I can't hear you. Are you there?

KATHY [*To Arny*]: I have a pressure and clenching around the heart.

Arny bends over her and helps her express what's happening inside of her.

ARNY: Show me the clenching. I will put my hand where yours is, and you clench my hand like the pressure around your heart.

Kathy grabs his hand and Arny nods.

Yes, harder. Now use both hands.

Kathy uses both hands to grab his. Her grip is strong.

Yeah, go on with that.

Kathy grabs Arny's hands and he resists ever so slightly to increase the feeling of grabbing. She suddenly shouts,

KATHY: *Speak up, Amy!* I can't hear you. Talk louder! Talk louder! I can't hear a word. Come closer! Get over here! [*Kathy is furious. She gets up and moves towards Amy. She reaches her hand out and screams.*] I WANT YOU TO COME CLOSER!

Amy still mutters softly, and Kathy, who is now next to Amy, drops her arm and looks paralyzed. She has reached another edge. Arny moves over to her and lifts one of her limp arms gently to feel what is in it. He recommends to her to feel her arm. Kathy rediscovers the furious and urgent feeling she just had.

I want to reach out, but it's so painful. [*She reaches out with one arm to Amy and smiles.*] Ha. It's not such a huge effort!

ARNY: No, it's just walking over. It touches you when you do that.

KATHY: Yes. I think I set it up to be such a huge effort. But it's much easier than I imagined. It's like the fear just went away. I would reach up, wanting my mom and dad to come and save me, and I realized they were not going to and I was just left out on a cliff. And I did not take care of myself. I just stopped. I did not realize I could just reach out.

*Beginning to
reach out*

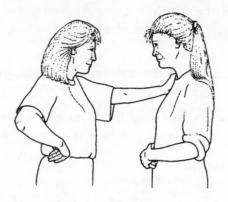

ARNY: Deafness amplifies your feeling of aloneness and challenges
   you to reach out. It's fascinating that reaching out is your secondary process. We can tell that it's secondary for many reasons, one of which is that someone did it for you in the
   beginning of the work by asking me to work with you. And
   then fate, the spin of the pen, chose you as well. I guess reaching out is your Tao, and ours as well, because when we spun
   the pen, it landed on you!

   Perhaps your work involves us all. Like you, we, too, will
   awaken from our dreaming and realize that we are dying of
   loneliness and need to reach out. [*To the group*] She was sleeping, knowing that she wasn't going to live forever and hoping
   her parents would make contact with her. But she woke up in
   the last minute. Remember her ritual? Light came in from
   above and she reached up, making shadow figures in the night.
   She has to do it herself. The ritual, dream and ear problem are
   all leading to the same conclusion. They are their own inter-
   pretations.

Working with Chronic Symptoms

SAM: Do you think that kids could already be conscious when
   they are little? Shouldn't parents realize children's needs? Why
   should Kathy have to reach out for herself?
ARNY: I don't have any ideas about what children or parents
   should do. I work with all of Kathy's parts, the kid who has

needs and the parent who neglects those needs. If Kathy were four years old and told me that dream, I would work with whatever was present. If she were an orphan, I would work with her and the community she lived in. If her parents brought her to me, I would work with the family system. If no one wanted to come with her and she had the dream of not being able to reach out, I might play with puppets. My only assumption is that everybody and everything which is present wants more awareness.

She worked with the symptom of deafness. A symptom is only the beginning of a process. It is only a state, a frozen process, which cannot unfold because of our edges to it. It is the beginning of a dream, a potential seed, waiting for the experience within it to unfold.

THERESA: You did something with her arm at one point.

ARNY: Yes, this is a specific aspect of movement work. Amy, would you help me with that? We'd like to show you something fun.

Amy and Arny come out to the center of the room. Amy is going to work with Arny's arm as a demonstration.

Let's say that I am making movements like Kathy, vibrating and shaking a bit, and then, suddenly, I drop it and put my arms down. At a certain moment the movement gets to an edge and I stop.

Although you stop, the movement you had been making is not gone. You can gain access to it again by moving the arm gently.

AMY: So now, I am going to lift Arny's arm and get into the dynamics of the dream in his muscles. The movement I am making with him is not the right one. It's not necessarily the movement that's inside him now, but by gently moving his arm, the potential movements in the static muscle will be accessed as they resist the wrong movement I am making.

I will try not to touch the fleshy part of the arm but only the bony part of the wrist. See, one of my hands is on his wrist, the other under the elbow. And very, very slowly I lift the arm.

Amy slowly lifts his arm upwards, and Arny, suddenly feeling what his arm wants to do, throws his arms wildly up in the air.

ARNY [*Gleefully*]: Wheee! I got it. It's this movement that's inside. I felt it right away.

He starts to do it again and stops, rubbing his head. Amy mirrors his arm motion, and Arny picks it up again, making noises with it.

Hmmhm. Yeah, yes. Now I know what these movements are. It's excitement! I'm trying to act like a cool teacher instead of showing my excitement! [*Arny jumps up and down like a kid, throwing his arms up excitedly. He then scratches his head.*] I want to say something and I have been shy or not able to.

AMY [*Encourages him*]: Go ahead! Experiment at the edge!

ARNY: It's hard. What I want to say is that Kathy's work excited me! It's OK if she is hard of hearing, but she doesn't have to be. She can have it if she needs it, but she can also do this other thing. She can pick up that whole process and reach out for people. It might just relieve the symptom.

Hmmm, I try to keep all these statements in so that I don't impose my own beliefs. I don't want to try to heal things which don't want healing. Thanks. [*Amy and Arny sit down.*] I shouldn't be a healer, but in fact I am interested in it! I've seen people reverse really serious symptoms and I tried to repress

Working with the arm

that information because I am afraid of being identified with being a healer. But that is in me too. It is exciting.

Catching the process can be life saving. It can make instantaneous physical changes. I remember once working with a woman who almost died from an allergy attack after being bitten by a bee. Then once during a seminar she was bitten by a bee again. She panicked, but this time asked me to help her.

I decided to pick up her secondary process, which is all we can ever do. I asked her what was wrong, and she said she had been poisoned, so I told her to be poisonous, to be as venomous as possible. I didn't care as much about the content of her poisonousness, but just the process. She screeched and screamed like a madwoman, and five minutes later sat down and forgot the bite.

Well, Amy, hmm, now working with my arm made me forget what we started to do. Oh yeah, getting stuck in movement. If someone gets stuck in movement, go ahead and move one of their arms and the structure that was in the muscles will still be there. All your movements are structured by the dreaming process in the muscles. Slow or "incorrect" movements that you do as the therapist give the client's movements a chance to express themselves. It's a blank access. By making a vague incomplete movement, you leave the muscles free to structure themselves and move in whatever way they will.

So, now, I'd like you to work on your chronic symptoms by amplifying and helping to complete processes. Then compare those processes with your childhood dreams or with a childhood memory. [*To one of the participants*] What symptoms will you work on?

SAM: Headaches.

ARNY: What kind of headaches?

SAM: Well, sometimes it's just there for three or four days.

ARNY [*To the group*]: Now watch and listen closely. I will use the sensory-grounded experience of a symptom as the intervention for working with it.

Arny asks Sam to describe the headache in such a way that Arny could feel it too.

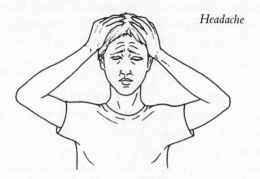

Headache

SAM [*Pauses*]: It starts like a tension right behind the eyes.

ARNY [*Nods, then inquires*]: Can you show me the tension with your hands?

Sam's hands make movements of pressure on his head.

> So that's how to work with that. Have him express his headache using his hand movements. Inner tension can be expressed outwardly very well. He should create pressure on himself and on other things and people, too.
>
> Someone tell me about another symptom.

JANET: Hypoglycemia.

ARNY: Yes, and how do you know that you are hypoglycemic?

Rising burning sensation

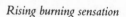

JANET: Because one of the symptoms is a rising sense of pain and burning from here up. [*She makes a hand motion indicating that the pain rises from her pelvis to her head.*]

ARNY: Beautiful. So to work with her you might use her hand motions. Be very careful when people describe symptoms. They always use medical terminology. That's not bad, but it's not too helpful. Medical terminology is based on pathological concepts which aim at chemical interventions. The medical descriptions are not individual descriptions of internal, sensory-grounded experience. When people describe a symptom, make sure that you can feel it, see it, hear it, sense it or relate to it too.

MAGGY: I have elevated pressure in the eyes.

ARNY: How does that feel?

MAGGY: There is no feeling.

ARNY: How do you know there is elevated pressure in your eyes?

MAGGY: I was told. It was measured. I take drops for it. You see, there's a history in the family of glaucoma, elevated eye pressure which eventually can cause deterioration.

ARNY: OK, so here's a special situation where she's experiencing a symptom in the moment, but relates the symptom instead to a family which has a tendency to go blind.

MAGGY: Well, my father did. This is not the same kind of thing he had, yet they said the pressure is creeping up.

ARNY: I'm not certain whether to go with the father going blind or the creeping pressure. Let me test the pressure. How do pressures creep up?

MAGGY: They describe it in terms of measurement.

ARNY: But why do you take the drops?

MAGGY: To relieve the pressure.

ARNY: So there's some pressure that's imagined in the background. You'd have to pretend that there's a pressure. Let's pretend there's a pressure inside of you. How would you give it expression? Express being pressured internally.

Maggy tenses up her face and shoulders.

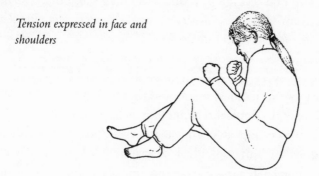

Tension expressed in face and shoulders

OK. That's how to work with it. There is the pressure. It looks like a strange face. The next thing to do would be to go on and work with it. Find out what that expression says. What's the story? For whom is the expression meant?

Maggy appears content with the information and says that she knows how to begin her work. Arny recommends that everyone sit in dyads and listen very closely to each other's descriptions of the symptoms. He stresses that it is important for the facilitator to feel and sense the client's symptoms before processing them further.

TERRY [*Suddenly raises her hand and asks*]: What about nausea and vomiting?

ARNY: What's it like to be nauseated? Could you give me a sensory-grounded experience of what it is like?

TERRY: Well, I'd have to throw up.

ARNY: Go ahead and do it.

TERRY [*Laughs*]: Not here!

ARNY [*Innocently*]: Well, why not throw up here?

TERRY [*Shocked by the suggestion*]: In public?

ARNY: But that's the point! Anyone can throw up privately.

Terry laughs.

Do you have something to throw up in public? Why not begin?

TERRY [*Stops and thinks for a moment*]: Oh, of course. You mean I have to express my negative opinions? Aha! I get it. Thanks.

PART III

Open Seat

CHAPTER 8

Process Work and Shamanism

The group gathers again in the evening after dinner. The day has been rich and full of powerful and intimate experiences. Though it has been only one day, it feels as if the group has been together for a long time. Arny starts the session talking about his and Amy's recent excursion to Africa.

The Open Seat and African Shamanism

ARNY: You know, being so introverted, I was always a little suspicious of working so openly with an individual in front of others. But Africa changed me. When Amy and I sat with the witch doctors in their hut, everybody was invited in. People from the village, the witch doctors, their apprentices, kids, the grandmothers, everyone was in on what I thought was supposed to be "our" healing. Moreover, the witch doctors not only worked with us, they had their own goals as well! They were training two of their apprentices, taking tumors out of their relatives, and perhaps most importantly of all, doing something for their tribe. The ritual itself, including the things they fished out of us, was, in fact, the central religious ceremony for their people. The wife was the seer; the husband, the hands-on healer; the son, the main helper; and all the rest of us were part of a loving, ecstatic and genuine experience.

Since that event, I understand my private practice as an important personal ritual, but I can also support working with individuals in public as a social or global ritual. In fact, I suspect that the work we will now do in the group, and our teaching, could be seen as redeveloping an ancient approach, as creating a modern ritual where the individual, couple or family which works is really a symbol for the spirit all of us feel.

JIM: Are you also referring to the "open seat" concept that the Gestalt trainers do here at Esalen?

ARNY: Yes and no. Fritz Perls, you know, left a "hot seat" or cushion in the circle for someone to work with. Then the most aggressive person, the one who reached the seat first, got the chance to work. Dick Price transformed that into a softer "open seat." I would like to keep the openness of the seat concept, but suggest changing the word "seat," because working with people involves so much movement. And I would also need to add a Taoistic flavor to the whole thing by not only asking the people who want to work, but also by spinning the pen to see which person chance chooses to work. Since chance is at work, we are working with the spirit of the moment or the group spirit.

AMY: This makes a lot of sense to me. I just recently dreamed that there was a whole group of Africans putting up a hut in which there was going to be an open seat! I guess they no longer wanted to focus on pure shamanism, but wanted to include the work we do here! It was beautiful. There was a huge setting sun and we were in the African bush.

ARNY: So let's make this evening a sort of cross-cultural "back to Africa!"

People laugh and agree.

Amy, remember Mombasa, and how much at home we felt in Africa? I feel that process work was developed there!

On Being Infected by the Client's Problems

LIZ: Before we get started, I wanted to ask you about the effects of this work on you as a therapist. Do you pick up the client's process and sometimes get sick?

ARNY: That's a very big question! There are a lot of different answers to that question. A shaman would say yes. If I get disturbed while working, I will work on myself in front of my client if she allows me to do so. This sort of inner work has its prototype in the shaman who goes in a trance to another world to help the client. If I start to get affected by someone, my main interest at that moment is to work on myself. Luckily, this almost always has a good effect upon the client. She sees I am human and usually feels more related to me, for I am no longer independent! There is no way out of such "counter-transference" situations. There is only a way in, and this is meaningful, because until this moment client and therapist have acted as if the client is the only one in the field.

Many times I get hurt by something a client unconsciously does. Then I notice how I first try to repress my hurt because I am not always in contact with my feelings. I'm just trying to act cool. But if I notice my feelings, I try to work on them in front of the person or even a whole group with the inner work methods we did this morning [*See Chapter 4*].

The fascinating thing is that the client is almost always unconscious of her hurtful radiation, and this apparent "hurtfulness" regularly turns out to be exactly what she needs to do even more, but consciously! So once I have gotten myself back on center, I frequently will try to help her to do the bothersome thing more consciously and more congruently. In this way, we both can grow and are grateful to each other, thank God!

To tell the truth, I am no longer worried about picking up affects or catching a physical disease from someone, because if I were to catch something, I would think that it must be something I need. You cannot get what you do not need to work on! I don't go looking for trouble. I try to care for myself physically as much as possible and, for some reason, don't pick up much psychic stuff anymore from others. But if I do, I try to integrate it immediately in the work.

Sometimes, I find myself getting dreamed up to be mediumistic, and have insights and knowledge which I cannot account for. I try to use the information for my own development and always share it with my client. Such situations usually happen when the client is shy about sharing something from her life.

BILL: In a work I did today I felt myself being very sad while I was working with someone. That was my response. What should I have done?

ARNY: Who knows? What did *you* do? Well, if I were you, I would have brought my sadness in. I would have said that I'm sad and asked the other person if he or she knew why. What is going on inside of you is an integral part of the other person's process. Frequently you are dreamed up, that is, you pick up experiences which the other person dreams about but has an edge against. Let me add, however, that if someone doesn't want his or her experiences, why not keep them for yourself? You must surely need them for something. You work the problems out. This is good shamanism and food for your personal psychology.

By the way, if you do work as a bodywork facilitator, don't just shake your hands and throw all the client's process into the universe. That could be bad ecology. No one knows where that stuff goes. If you are infected by the client's problems, work on them in yourself either internally or out loud.

We don't know much about our psychic systems, but I'm not sure it's right to throw junk into the universe. I think it's better to process or recycle your perceptions and all the stuff that you pick up. If you throw out all that aggression and unhappiness, it might go right down the street and into somebody who can't take it.

SHELLY: So how do you know what is their process and what's yours?

ARNY: This depends upon your personal viewpoint. I don't think a process really belongs to any one person. We pick up parts of the huge field we all live in. Whoever sees, hears, feels, or senses anything should be thankful for these perceptions and try to use them for themselves and others as much as possible. In this way, everything is me, and nothing is me.

Everyone falls silent for a few moments. Arny works rapidly with four different people in the next hour. Two are described in this chapter and two in the next.

Fighting Diabetes

ARNY [*Looks around*]: Now, enough theory, how should we decide who wants to work?

Many people raise their hands. Arny nods.

There are lots of people who want to work. Should we spin the pen? Let's make a group decision about that. Annie was about to work this afternoon.

The group unanimously agrees that Annie should work. Annie gets up and meets Arny in the center of the circle. They stand facing each other. Arny waits silently.

ANNIE: Arny, I'd like to work on a childhood dream and also on my diabetes and on a liver problem. Should I tell you the dream?

ARNY [*Nods*]: Go ahead. [*He quickly goes and gets a piece of paper to write on.*]

ANNIE: I had this dream several times when I was a child and the dream was...

Arny starts to sit down on the floor to write down her dream, but Annie continues to stand. The group starts to laugh.

ARNY: That's negative feedback! See, I wanted to sit but she wasn't going with it. That's not where she is. Standing and telling dreams is where she is. Oh, well. This may be a part of her work.

ANNIE: The dream is that I am in a yard in my childhood home. I hear music coming from some place that I don't know, a mandolin type music. Then I see a large black falcon or hawk

carrying something and standing off in profile. And I am filled
with fear and I just stand there.

ARNY: Ah, standing there, here? Out of fear? A falcon, yes. Diabetes, hmm... but what is diabetes?

ANNIE: Tiredness, hunger, thirst, poor eyesight.

ARNY: Hmm. How long have you had diabetes?

ANNIE: The last three years.

She has described the diabetes so far by listing symptoms that
could be associated with a number of diseases. Arny wants to have
a more sensory-grounded description of how she experiences her
diabetes. Therefore he asks: "Why don't you try to give me diabetes?"

ANNIE [*Astounded*]: Give you diabetes?

ARNY [*Playfully*]: Well, why not? Let's say I am going around in
my life and you give me diabetes.

He starts to walk around the room. Annie just watches, giggles,
and then walks over to him. Using her hands, she very firmly
pushes him down to the floor. He gently resists, but she puts him
down again. In fact, she almost sits on him. He tries to sit up
again, while simultaneously encouraging her.

ARNY: Go on, you're doing just beautifully. I never had diabetes
like that!

She and the group laugh.

Diabetes-maker

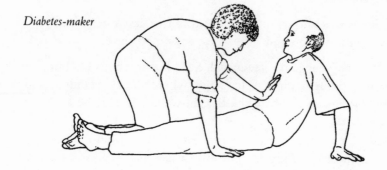

ANNIE [*Laughing*]: It's fun. [*She looks a bit surprised at her own enjoyment.*]

ARNY [*Joins her mood*]: It's fun to give diabetes, isn't it? Let's have fun.

Annie continues to push him down, resisting his struggle to get up.

ANNIE: Stay there!

ARNY [*Tries to provoke her*]: I should stay here?

ANNIE [*Pauses*]: Well, you can get up, but slowly! I don't want you to move very much.

Arny stands up and then jumps up and down. Annie holds his arms.

No, no. Not too much.

ARNY: Show me how to move. Show me the kinds of movements you would like me to make. I liked when you held my arms. I want you to go ahead and enjoy yourself, be creative, and I want you to tell me how you want me to move.

Still as the diabetes-maker, Annie says, "Like this." She begins to walk very slowly, hanging her head and slouching her shoulders. Her legs are dragging heavily on the floor. Arny starts to mirror her, walking exactly as she does. As she walks in this way, she is organically switching roles. She is leaving the role of the creator of diabetes, and becoming the victim, the one with the diabetes. She unconsciously changes here because the experience of the victim of the disease has not been completed.

Go ahead and show me. You're doing great. Really trudge along.

She increases the heaviness of her walk. Her head flops forward and she steps harder on her feet. With each step her body sways forward. She looks as if she is about to collapse.

ARNY [*Impressed*]: That's strong. [*He turns to the rest of the group.*] Look at her in movement. Keep your eyes on her. [*He does the movement with her, and speaks to her.*] I'd like to show you what you're doing. Take a look at me and tell me what you see me doing.

Annie stops and studies the movements Arny is making.

ANNIE: I see. I am dying of thirst in a desert.
ARNY: Oh. I wouldn't have known that.

Annie now moves more and more slowly. She falls to her knees, then to the ground on all fours. She is crawling on the ground, barely able to move.

ANNIE: I've got to keep going, to find water.

She crawls on slowly, straining and dragging her body with her arms. She stops every now and then, looks at Arny, and goes on. She looks like she's carrying a huge weight. Suddenly she collapses onto her side. She makes an attempt to pull herself up, but collapses again. Arny sits down now. They are about six feet apart.

I can see the desert. I don't see any water.
ARNY: I don't see any water either. What a spot to be in. She's in the desert with no water. This is really something.
ANNIE: Well, I have to keep going.

Arny wants to provoke the part of her which goes on. He wants to encourage her to fight for life.

ARNY: Is that right? I didn't realize you wanted to live. How would I know that besides the change in your movement?

Dying of thirst

ANNIE: Because I have to find water or die.

ARNY: Because you have to find water or die. Well, are you sure you want to find water? Are you sure you don't want to die?

Annie starts to crawl again, then pauses as he asks her the question.

ANNIE: No, I want to live.

ARNY [*Quietly*]: I believe it, almost.

Annie starts to crawl around again, a little faster. Arny stands up and looks around as if searching for her. She is behind him. He looks up and down and then backs up a bit. She pauses. The situation seems tense and uncertain.

ARNY: You're thinking. Remember that you have the keys which can help. Just become aware of whatever is happening inside of you and follow it. What are you thinking?

ANNIE: I'm thinking that there *must* be a way out of the desert.

ARNY: That "must" is the key. [*Challenging*] Really? I don't see anything, I just can't find the way out.

Annie laughs.

Interesting thing to laugh about. I enjoy that. Let's laugh together about no way out. What a spot to be in and what a reaction! What's funny?

ANNIE: It's not really funny. Why am I doing all this dying and struggling?

ARNY: Don't you want to die?

ANNIE: I was afraid of that. [*She looks down at her hands, playing with her fingers.*]

ARNY: Your eyes changed. Are you sad?

Annie nods and starts to cry, keeping her head down. Arny asks her compassionately if she wants to die. She shakes her head and assures him, "I don't want to die."

ARNY: Right, some people have an edge to living. [*He starts to push her down again.*] I'll be the thing holding you down. Just lie down!

Annie starts to cry, but then pushes back. She grabs his leg to make him fall to his knees, and continues to fight with him. They both

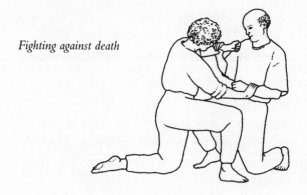

Fighting against death

struggle on the ground and she finally manages to push him force-fully onto his back on the floor.

> What are you doing with me? I am diabetes, trying to push you down and you are supposed to die!

ANNIE: No, you're supposed to die!

ARNY: Me? I'm not dying. I am the killer!

They struggle again briefly. Arny gives her resistance, but she suddenly shoves him so strongly that he's flat out on his back. He scrambles up to a sitting position.

ANNIE [*Laughs*]: It was fun, the fighting!

ARNY [*Laughing*]: Yes, fighting is fun but submitting is no fun!

Annie is laughing now and nods at what Arny is saying. He continues to test her newfound determination.

> You mean you don't want to just lie down and die? You want to fight for your life?

ANNIE [*Confidently*]: Yeah!

ARNY: I thought so.

They both laugh and Annie makes a determined face.

ARNY: I like the way you looked at me!

He mirrors it and shows her what she was doing. Annie makes the face again.

ANNIE [*Very quietly, but powerfully*]: Don't mess with me. [*Repeating it louder*] Don't mess with me! [*She pushes him back.*]

ARNY: Who are you that I shouldn't mess with you?

ANNIE: I'm a person.

ARNY: Yeah, but we gods decide who is going to live and who is going to die on this planet. So just go ahead and die. We command everyone, except certain characters like you don't obey.

ANNIE: I have a mind of my own, too. I don't have to listen all the time to everything the gods say.

She pushes him all the way down to the floor and laughs. Arny stands up and shoves her back playfully. She falls over laughing and they hug for a moment.

ARNY [*Exclaims*]: I like you like this!

ANNIE: [*Nods; she looks happy and thoughtful*]: It's true. I take the treatment that I get without fighting back. Yeah, thank you.

They laugh together, embrace and leave the center of the circle.

Discussion

ARNY [*To the group*]: Isn't that interesting? The diabetes was like a predatory bird, going after its prey, putting her down. Diabetes challenges her to be equally as strong as it is, and not follow the rules or fates given by others.

The hawk from Annie's dream lives inside of her. There are a lot of people who feel that their lives are threatened because they are constantly challenged by something like these powerful birds, which are their secondary processes. Only under the threat of death do they meet the bird and integrate it by fighting for the right to live and battle fate. Only when you have to go into the greatest of all battles do you become the heroine that you are.

Her primary experience, or normal identity, is to feel exhausted and depressed. Her secondary process as she first described it in medical terms is called diabetes. But, in truth, her diabetes is a kind of secret ally, a disease which challenges her to overcome it and truly live. The trick is that only by being pushed all the way down, going all the way into that exhaustion, could she make the next big step and live.

[*Arny pauses and looks around.*] Well, what are we going to do next?

Everyone says he should spin the pen. He spins the pen and it points to Greg.

Accessing the Children's Savior

GREG: Good. I'd like to work. I felt I was working in all the processes today. I was working on chronic pain in the back and around my heart. I want to check out this pain that I've had for years. I want it to go away, or to do something to transform it.

Arny begins to walk towards Greg, but surprisingly and unexpectedly begins to hop like a rabbit. He jumps from a crouching position, keeping his feet together and using his hands to push himself up.

ARNY: I noticed I just hopped.

Greg nods.

And I can't figure out why on earth I'm hopping. Maybe you can help me with it. Excuse me for interrupting you. What is all this about? [*Arny goes back to his original place and begins again. This time he hops forward slowly, in a movement meditation. He stops hopping and turns to Greg*]: Do you know what this hopping is about?

GREG: I have a sneaking suspicion.

ARNY: Do you ever hop?

GREG [*Giggles*]: Well, it's not so much hopping that I do…

As he talks, he begins to crouch over and hops towards Arny. Suddenly a mad scene ensues. They're both hopping around the room while everyone laughs. Greg swings his arms loosely as he hops.

It's more like an ape.

Greg now swings his body like an ape. He sits on his back legs, sways back and forth, and begins to beat his chest, like Tarzan. He looks up at Arny, who grins at him. Greg actually looks like an

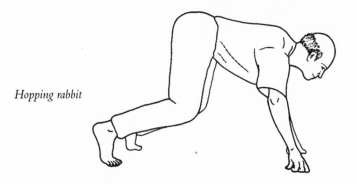

Hopping rabbit

ape. After a while, Arny too bends over and begins to swing his arms. Greg gets up on his feet, and bounces and hops around the room, with his arms hanging loosely at his sides. Arny gives a huge sigh of relief.

GREG [*Pants for breath*]: I think my heart hurts because I don't do this ape thing enough!

People laugh wildly.

ARNY [*Nods*]: Yeah, some things are very simple. You don't do this enough?

Arny gets up and shows him how he looked as an ape. Greg begins to bounce around again.

GREG: Right, it's like letting my chest just… [*He beats his chest with his fist and lets out a huge Tarzan-like call.*]

The apes

The group laughs hysterically. Greg rubs his head, suddenly very shy, and hides in a corner.

ARNY [*Laughs*]: I like that movement. How did it go?

Greg hits his chest again, screaming like Tarzan. People burst into laughter. Arny imitates Greg's movements and sounds. Greg scampers off and then returns. He comes up to Arny and they hold hands and swing their arms.

GREG: You know, that's inside me, but I don't give myself permission to do it in public very often. I don't see why, though. This is the problem.

ARNY: We'll soon find out. Just one more step? Is it possible?

Arny imitates him, beating on his chest and making monkey sounds. Greg starts again. He crouches over, keeping low to the ground. He prowls around the room, using his "paws" to propel himself. His growls get louder and stronger.

Yeah, that's the growl I'm looking for. Go on with movement as if you were doing an art form. Forget psychology. Just let your body create a story.

Greg continues to growl. He stands up on his "hind" feet. Arny turns to him and growls, "Yeah, gggrraaarrrggghhh. You're growling about something. Yeah?" Greg pushes as Arny now makes animal sounds. He's still swinging his arms like an ape. Arny reaches over and gently inhibits one of his arms. By stopping the movement, he's encouraging Greg to go deeper into the movement impulse.

Greg makes a fist and puts it in Arny's hand. Suddenly Greg looks completely serious, and withdraws his arm. He puts his fist back out.

GREG: This fist means "Don't fucking mess with me."

ARNY [*Nods*]: Aha. So there's a figure behind the ape. Don't fucking mess with who? Yes, with, about, when... yeah?

Greg is surprised by himself. He pauses for a moment and almost begins to cry. Seeing that Greg is at an edge, Arny touches his hand, hoping to find the movement in the arm again. He prompts Greg.

"Don't fucking mess with me." The ape was talking to someone. What's the myth, the story or memory?

GREG: Well, I'm getting an image of Nazis killing babies. I don't know how this relates to me.

ARNY: Yeah, I don't know what I know either. Yeah. Nazis killing babies. OK. This is a bad scene. We should create and finish that up. [*Hesitating*] How does it look? Do you have a vision?

GREG: Well, the image that came up was an experience that my mother had.

ARNY: Yes, OK. This is your mother's work. What was it?

GREG: She was in Europe... in the war. The Nazis came on board her boat... and there was a baby on the ship and... the baby died. She killed her own baby before the... before the soldiers could. The baby died.

ARNY: OK. So here's the scene. There's somebody over here [*Pointing to a spot in the room*]. Would somebody come out and help me here?

A woman volunteers.

Thank you. Could you be the mother with the baby? Hold this pillow as if it were your baby. And you, Greg, will you be... the protector?

[*Arny starts to play the Nazi.*] OK. Who's on board here? Anybody got a baby? What's going on here on this ship?

He stomps around, looking and sounding tough. Greg goes up to the mother, puts his hand on her shoulder, and tells her to be quiet. Arny, playing the Nazi, comes over to where they're standing.

So, there's a baby over there? [*He turns to the mother.*] Give it to me. No babies allowed here. [*He reaches toward the baby. As he approaches, Greg holds Arny back. Arny turns to Greg.*] Who are you?

GREG [*Looks tough*]: Don't fucking mess around, man. [*Greg uses his whole body to push Arny further back to the edge of the circle. Arny encourages him to go on.*] I'll fucking kill you unless you get the hell out of here right now. I'm going to kill you anyway. [*Greg is standing over Arny, whom he has pushed down to the floor. He speaks threateningly.*] Are you going to leave or do I have to kill you?

ARNY: I'm going. When you're like this, I can go.

Greg nods. He looks as if he's relieved and has understood something. He stands up and Arny sits up and looks at him.

ARNY: I like that part of you. I think you inhibit that monkey too much. There is a protector behind him. But let's go further with the protector. You don't let it live enough. I want you to do that. There must be a lot of things that you need to stand up for. The first is your own hopping around, your own child. There is the inner Nazi who kills the kid in you. What about an outer story? Something outside to stand up for?

GREG [*Nods*]: Yes. There's a lot to stand up for.

ARNY [*Looks serious*]: Do you want to say something? I'll listen. Be my teacher and tell me what to stand up for.

GREG: Well, the main thing is to stand up against ignorance, against idiots like the Nazis who just destroy life with stupid ideas. And there's also love to stand up for. And the fact that we are all one and we don't have to kill ourselves.

Arny bows to Greg and they stand silently looking at each other for a moment. Greg looks down to the right. Arny points there.

ARNY: You had a thought?

Greg burps and everyone laughs. Arny and Greg embrace. Arny yells, "Long live the child!"

Discussion

Arny and Greg sit back down in the circle and Arny discusses the work with the others.

ARNY: It's interesting. The movement he began with looked like a playful ape, but there was something about the ape's movements that wasn't just playful. His voice didn't sound like he was playing a game. That ape was the beginning of his aggression against the child killer.

TERRY: You just followed yourself, though. You found yourself hopping and just followed it.

ARNY: Yeah, perhaps his beginning seriousness dreamed me up to be so playful. As soon as he began to worry about his symptoms, something in me responded with hopping. Perhaps I unconsciously picked up the signals of the ape or the child he was protecting.

On the other hand, that hopping thing could just have been me. When I work, I am who I am. The other is whoever he is, and what belongs to me or the other doesn't matter. If you find yourself hopping or if you find yourself doing anything at all why not just follow it? You can start anywhere, with yoga, with your hands, with meditation, or with your own feelings and impulses. Everything is an entry point into the river which goes its own way.

You must experiment with being yourself! Try starting anywhere, with any aspect of your creativity, knowledge, or interests. How you work as a facilitator is a complex mixture of your real self, your client, the relationship between the two of you, and the universe.

It even seems that if a client works with two process-oriented facilitators, he will get the same insights and results if both facilitators truly follow themselves as well as the client's feedback and process. Where you start and how you work is unpredictable and individual, but where you go depends upon the nature of the client.

Some process workers prefer beginning with thinking. Some like to play, but in another mood, they will think. Let's think. Remember the beginning of Greg's work? His movement wasn't completely occupied. I think he said he wanted his symptoms to "go away," as if they could have a motion of their own. Thus, if you like to think, you might have thought that since movement was not consciously occupied, an intervention with movement might have been a useful way to get started. So you can think, but sometimes it is the most fun to begin by playing.

DAVE: That was impressive, all that primal masculine energy.

GREG: Right. Well, my mother was afraid for me to be that powerful. She herself wanted to be invisible and avoid the Germans until she could escape from Europe.

ARNY: I understand and appreciate that. But that is also how she herself smothered the baby. She understandably and yet unconsciously entered into collusion with the tyrant when she tried to be invisible. That is how all minorities inadvertently side with the persecutor. They treat themselves in the same hurtful way that the oppressor treats them. It's absolutely wicked. But you just turned it around.

CHAPTER 9

More Open Seat

Without another word of explanation, Arny turns to the other side of the room.

ARNY: Laura, you've had your hand up over there, I see. Should I work with you, or should I work with somebody else? [*He turns to the rest of the group.*] Should I work with Laura, or should we spin the pen to choose who works next?

The group agrees that Arny should work with Laura. Laura also says quietly that she would be happy to work with Arny. She gets up, walks across the room to where Arny is sitting, and sits down. Before she has time to say anything, Arny gets up.

ARNY: Did I catch you walking like this?
[*He stands up and imitates her walk. He walks very softly and tentatively, as if on tiptoe.*]

Laura is shocked at first at the suddenness of Arny's intervention. But after a moment, she too gets up and starts to tiptoe around the room with him. They both look like they are doing movement improvisation. The group is laughing and enjoying this unconventional beginning. As they continue to tiptoe, Laura starts to use her hands, raising them slightly, a combination of fearful and stalking

Tiptoeing

motions. After a few minutes of this, with both Arny and Laura enjoying themselves immensely, Arny turns to Laura.

ARNY: What are we doing? Have you any idea?
LAURA [*Nods*]: This is how I am. Something might happen.

Arny seizes upon her statement, "Something might happen." He sees in it a "blank access;" the lack of content indicates that he could use it as a technique to find out more about the movements she is making.

ARNY: Yes, if we are not cautious, some very specific *thing* might happen!

Laura looks puzzled, but agrees.

Arny walks beside Laura as they tiptoe around the circle. He tip-toes in an obviously secretive, cautious way. Every now and then he looks around, over his shoulder, as if he's watching for something scary or dangerous. The people in the group are laughing uproariously at their pantomime.

Arny speaks in a very comic tone, exaggerating the melodrama of the pantomime.

If we are not quiet, we could wake that damn thing up! For God's sake, don't laugh too loudly. You never know *who's* around here or what could happen. Something might happen, you know. Something definitely could happen. What could be the worst thing that could happen? Tell me. I promise I won't tell anybody else.

Laura shrugs, indicating that she doesn't know.

You can't imagine something awful, can you? Should I imagine something awful? I am imagining something awful. Do you know what I imagine? Take a guess!

Everyone laughs at his trickster-like and playful manner, and at his obvious attempt to get her to project what she knows.

Watch and guess. Watch me. Your job is to guess what it is I'm afraid of.

Laura stands and watches Arny as he tiptoes fearfully around the room. She looks thoughtful.

LAURA: Hmm. Well, I see that I'm afraid. I don't want to look stupid.
ARNY: You don't want to look stupid to... you-know-whom is looking!
LAURA: Her.
ARNY: Who?
LAURA: Mary.

Though Arny has no idea who Mary is, he encourages Laura to play the critical figure by whom she feels observed. It is important to Arny to follow this flow of events, that is, to have Laura enact this figure, rather than find out the details about Mary at this stage.

ARNY: Go ahead and play Mary. Just watch me playing you, and you play the critical Mary. [*As Laura*] Mary, is that you?

While playing Laura, Arny whispers out of the corner of his mouth, encouraging Laura to play Mary, but Laura is afraid to play this figure. So Arny switches roles and plays Mary, the critical observer. Since he has no idea who she is, but only knows that Laura feels observed by her, he improvises. Arny speaks in a different voice.

My name is Mary, and you are a puny thing. You woke me up. Shut up and be quiet while you walk. You tried to be quiet and get around me, but I am always here. That's better, be quiet. Disappear and go behind the curtains.

As he speaks, Laura gets depressed and steps away a bit.

LAURA: I don't want to. Forget Mary.

ARNY: An edge. Should I just forget this? No, I can't let go of it yet.

LAURA: I want to get out of this, whatever is next.

ARNY [*Persisting*]: Laura, just play Mary for one minute, twenty seconds. I'll make a deal with you. Go ahead and just do it. Play her.

Arny's persistence works. Laura very slowly begins to play the figure of Mary. She turns to Arny, addressing him as if he were her.

LAURA: Can't you be less idealistic?

ARNY: You are doing great. [*Now in the role of the fearful Laura*] I am an idealistic flower.

LAURA: Why not get a job? You have your stupid Ph.D. now!

ARNY: I should get a job? I didn't know that you were interested in my life.

LAURA: Well, at least you should look good.

Arny encourages Laura to continue playing Mary.

ARNY: Go ahead, play it. Pretend this is a game, have fun.

Laura stands up stiffly, and strikes a tyrannical pose. Arny looks up at her.

Mary, is that you? Tell me what to do. Direct my life. What would you like?

LAURA [*Hesitates*]: I'm trying to get a sense of her.

Arny begins to move away, noticing out of the corner of his eye that Laura is still standing in a stiff pose like Mary. She suddenly stands up straight, pulls her head back, sticks out her shoulders, and grunts.

LAURA [*Haughtily*]: I do hope you find a job right now. We're back here waiting.

ARNY: Who is we?

LAURA [*Still as Mary*]: The kids, the family. What are you doing out there?

ARNY [*Takes a guess into Laura's life*]: Spiritual things.

LAURA [*Looks down at him with disdain*]: Your things are a waste of time. Going to church. Your thing is ridiculous. You should just stop hanging around out there. You should be married and have a husband.

Still not knowing anything about her life, Arny takes a wild guess.

ARNY: Well, I have something like a husband.

Everyone bursts out laughing.

LAURA: Where?

Arny repeats her question and looks around rather sheepishly. Laura laughs at him.

ARNY: OK, I'll get a husband.

LAURA: It's too late now. You should get a job and use your degree.

Arny notices that she uses her index figure to point with. He gently grasps her finger, sculpting her hand into a directive gesture, hence somatically recommending her to use this finger in her dialogue.

Use all your knowledge, all those years of studying. Use your degree. You are wasting your talents.

Sculpting Laura's finger

ARNY: Go on.

Laura continues, embodying the figure of Mary more strongly. She is taking up the role more congruently and at the same time transforming the figure slightly, from a purely nasty one to one with useful criticisms.

LAURA: You have all the resources in you to do it, and you want to do it and [*Louder*] you are good at it. Who cares about the stupid license right now? Don't worry about the rules. [*Yelling*] Just keep doing it now, like you are doing it with the clients you already have! [*To Arny*] This is really me talking, more than anything else. [*She speaks again as the role.*] Well, you do not have any personal life.
ARNY [*Continuing as Laura*]: What should I do?
LAURA [*Laughing and pointing with her index finger*]: You have a terrible life right now.

Arny moves closer to her and touches her pointing finger to awaken her awareness so she can continue being Mary.

How can you go on in your life if you do not have a personal life! Intimacy is your big problem. You belong to the human race for Chrissakes!
ARNY: Laura, I didn't know that you had this teacher inside. [*Arny shows her the teacher by standing up as she did, pointing her finger. He then turns to the group.*] Will someone make notes for Laura so she won't forget the teachings of this part? Would someone please help us and repeat back what the teacher said?
STEVE [*To Laura*]: You are good at what you do.
ARNY [*As the teacher*]: You are good at what you do. Forget about the license.
RON [*To Laura*]: Keep doing what you are doing with your clients.
ARNY: Keep on with your clients. Get over this intimacy barrier. Do it with anyone, with everyone. Have a good time.
PAM: Use the talents you have. You have resources inside your self.

Laura nods and moves closer to Arny. She thanks him and they hug.

ARNY: I love your critical energy, the Mary figure. She has the clues.

Arny and Laura go back to their places in the circle and sit down again.

LAURA: I just became aware of the group. I just realized that I'm part of the group here.

Arny thinks to himself that the critical figure, Mary, is probably projected onto the group. He imagines that Laura has flipped back to the fearful personality and is feeling timid in the group.

ARNY: What did you become aware of in the group?

LAURA: I wanted to ask something. Did they...

PARTICIPANT: We liked your new powerful voice.

ARNY: I liked your Mary. Do you need anything more from the group? Is everything completed now?

LAURA [*No longer timid, but bold*]: YES! Thanks!

ARNY [*Pauses, and then says to the group*]: When you begin to get into an inner figure like Mary, the figure transforms. In Laura's case, it became a useful teacher. It is actually a part of Laura, and the original designation, Mary, was no longer valid. That is process work; we focus on the process, not just the original designation. If we were talking quantum physics, we would say we are working with the wave as well as the particle description of nature.

Amy's Flowchart

During Laura's work Amy sketched a chart that plots the way processes evolve. This flowchart follows the course of the process, which is constantly changing.

In the beginning of every work the way we identify ourselves, our primary process, seems fairly clear. Then, as the work progresses and we begin to pick up what has been further from consciousness and experience more of the original secondary process, our identity changes and we no longer identify with our original selves. We transform, and get a new primary process. At that moment of new identity, yet another new and

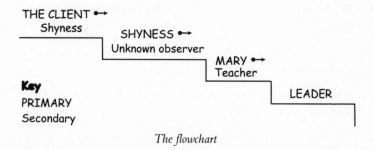

The flowchart

unpredictable something appears on the distant horizon, and we have a new secondary process to become conscious of. And on it goes!

Amy's chart follows these changes and stresses the fluid and changing nature of who we are. It shows our ability to identify with awareness, rather than only with momentary states, and charts the different identities to which we attach ourselves as we transform throughout the day and through our lives.

In Laura's work, she was first just a simple client interested in working on herself, and her shy movements were a secondary process [See diagram on this page]. As Laura identified with her shyness, the unknown observer became the secondary process with which she could not identify. She had an edge to take over this role, but when she did, deep inside the negative observing figure of Mary was a true inner guide or teacher. When Laura picked up the role of the teacher, the work came to a temporary end. At that moment, she was congruent, her whole self, a leader, waiting for the process of change to challenge her once again to become more and more of herself.

The Search for Love

ARNY: Well, we have a couple of minutes yet. Perhaps someone has a small problem at this point. Does anyone have something to work on?

A young woman, Linda, raises her hand.

LINDA: I have a problem. Can I work on it?

ARNY: Sure.

LINDA: Can you work on dreams without bodywork? I have had recurring dreams for the last few days. Can we just work on it verbally without bodywork?

ARNY: Yes, you can do anything with dreams that feels right. Tell us your dream.

Arny thinks to himself that Linda's interest in doing dreamwork without bodywork may indicate that she feels shy about body experiences. She probably has an edge about them, and thus they may play an important role here.

LINDA: In the last five months I have been dreaming about penises. They appear in different ways and in different shapes. In one dream I am locked in the bathroom and when I open the door, a gigantic man with this huge penis appears and he starts to pee all over me. I run away and he begins to run after me. I get my brother, but my brother begins to kiss this man passionately.

In another dream I was with this man with whom I just finished a relationship. We are naked and playing, and our bodies are against each other, like three of my dreams have been about the same thing with him. We wanted to have intercourse and he stopped. But I can just feel his penis against me and that is my focal point, and I wake up.

ARNY: What did you say about focal point?

LINDA: What?

ARNY: What did you hear?

LINDA: What a focus this penis is.

People laugh.

Why would I focus on something which is dicking me around so much?

ARNY [*Jokingly*]: Well, let's talk about penises in general. Do you like them?

LINDA: I'm not willing to give them up.

People laugh again.

I think the thing I keep hearing is that men dick you around. Whenever there is a penis involved, it always ends up hurting.

ARNY: Oh, I'm sorry about that. You might enjoy trying to be a dream penis. Did you ever try that?

Linda and everyone in the room laugh at the suggestion.

LINDA: No. [*Joking*] That could be a peak experience. Sure. Do you have any suggestions how to do that?

ARNY: Let's just have fun right now.

LINDA: If I were a penis, I'd need to rub up against the whole group!

The group laughs. Linda gets up and starts moving around. She bends down and rubs up against one participant after another, using her head. She moves around the circle this way, spending about a minute with each participant. After having gone about halfway around the circle, Linda stops.

I thought at first I would not even get up.

She begins to sit back down, and Arny stops her by saying,

ARNY: Want to try one more?

Arny stands up and meets her in the center of the room. She moves towards him and they fluidly begin a movement improvisation. They rub heads, rocking back and forth. They twist and turn around their heads and then start to rub their backs together. Arny follows her lead. They start to bend and roll, while still standing on their feet.

Their hands dangle and swing. He puts one arm half around her shoulders, then urges her, without speaking, to take the initiative. She begins to circle around him. He moves slowly, letting her determine the improvisation. She bends over and encircles him. Suddenly Linda stands up and stops.

LINDA: I want to stop. I just had the urge to get inside of you.

Arny understands that she got to an edge in movement. He does not focus on the content of her statement, but rather on the sudden break in the flow of movement.

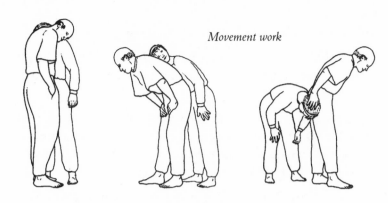

Movement work

ARNY: Why not experiment with doing it? Over the other side of the edge is rarely what you think.

Linda [*Shocked*]: Oh! How?

Arny doesn't answer her, but understanding that she came to an edge in movement, starts to move again with her. They swing about, then she twists around so that she is behind him. She bends down and puts her head between his legs.

He twists around and then bends forwards over her back. He is leaning over her and his stomach is on her back. They both sink to their knees in this position. She lets go and falls limply to the ground. Arny remains sitting, cradling her now in his lap. He puts his arms around her. She cries softly, breathing deeply, and then both are still.

Arny and Linda stay in that position for a few minutes. After a long silence they both slowly sit up and look at each other. Everyone else is quietly touched and looks on.

They sit close to one another, both looking at the floor. Sometimes they glance up at each other for a moment, but they mostly play shyly with something on the carpet. Everyone remains silent.

ARNY: We do not have to talk. Some things do not have to be spoken about. Is that OK?

Linda nods. She seems deep in thought. She looks at Arny.

Do you remember what you were feeling down there?

LINDA: Yes.

ARNY: Fine, OK. We'll talk about it when the time is right.

> [Later that evening, Linda told us that she found herself searching for and finding a missing father in the work with Arny.]

Linda moves closer to Arny and gives him a hug. They part, both going back to their original places in the circle. The group sits in silence for another minute, affected by the atmosphere generated by the work. After a while, someone speaks.

HENRY: Arny, that was really touching. I would have been afraid of body contact. I mean, gosh... do you ever think of sex?

ARNY: Sexuality is a very important experience unto itself, but in process work it almost always appears as just one more state in the incredible spectrum of fluid transformations. Bringing awareness into what we thought was a static frozen state, an idea or a dream image like a penis, releases it and allows it to unfold, revealing depths and meanings which we could scarcely intuit.

The more you work with your body feeling, your proprioception and your movement, the more familiar and fluid these avenues of expression become, and the less you fear them or get possessed by any of their states. Many of you bodyworkers may already know what I mean. Unused channels like body feeling or movement are like dreams for us. But a dream

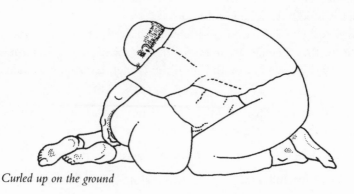

Curled up on the ground

is, after all, only the beginning state of a process; it is but one picture of a dreaming world. Process work, like movement improvisation, focuses on the dreaming process, the stream of creativity and change which reveals the deepest messages and creates the most unexpected experience.

After the discussion, everyone is quiet. Then Arny looks up and says, "Let's meet at 9:30 tomorrow morning." He places his hands in an honoring gesture to the group and stands up. Someone says, "Thanks."

PART IV

World Work

CHAPTER 10

Relationship Work

O n the last morning of the seminar the participants stroll around and find their spots in the circle. Arny begins working by asking the participants about their dreams from the night before.

ARNY: Good morning. What kind of things happened in the night? I don't want to work in detail on dreams, but I just like hearing dreams when I wake up. [*Arny pauses and waits for a response. No one volunteers to tell a dream.*]

Well, I myself had a big dream. Should I tell my dream? I don't dream often, but last night I dreamed I was en route to finding the ancient mystery of the American Indians. I've studied them, but in the dream it was a real trek. And to find the Native American treasure on this trek you have to have the right eyes to see the clues.

The clues were on ancient engraved stones which were lying around. Other people hadn't seen them yet. The clues were carved engravings, like Aztec symbols, and they had Chinese clocks on them. Have you ever seen a Chinese clock? It's a labyrinth. In order to find the treasure, you had to see these little tiny stones with labyrinths engraved in them. I saw them and could follow the ancient stones, and it was a very exciting thing. I went from one point to the next, finding first this clue and then that, like a treasure hunt!

Suddenly, at one point in the dream, I became different kinds of people. I was an old man, a woman and then a child. As a child I went along the beach and other children came behind me and we were all on a treasure hunt. And finally, believe it or not, we actually found the treasure! We finally got to the treasure. It was a bag. And everyone sat around the bag and now the treasure of the American Indians, the essence of America, was going to come out, and we would unravel it. How exciting!

It wasn't me but a woman who was opening the bag. The treasure had to do with life and death. Apparently the Native Americans had long ago discovered the art of bringing the dead back to life! And, by God, when this woman opened the bag, inside the bag was the secret of the Indians. Apparently this woman's father or relative had died years ago and they had brought him back to life! His head was alive!

She opened the bag and there was a living head sewn onto a puppet's body. This living face looked at her and said "Hello," and she fainted. That was the end of the dream. That's what happened to me last night. A renewed tribal spirit, the old father or ancient spiritual principle!

MAGGY: I don't know if you are aware of the event which will occur on August 16 or 17, a couple of days away, the so-called Harmonic Convergence. It's all about the Aztec and Mayan prophecies coming together on that date, and ancient spirits coming back to earth.

ARNY: Spirits, hmm. The eternal in us, in me. An eternal principle, with its own mind, but we give it life and body... hmm. The tribal aspect is important, whether America, Africa, or wherever.

I suddenly think of Black Elk's dream of a new tribal ritual to renew the spirit of his family. Our tribe is dying, too. The tribal life on our planet is dying. Our world is speeding into the twenty-first century. Does my dream say anything useful?

The Chinese clocks on the stones and clues in the dream remind me of sensory-grounded awareness, giving us the direction to the treasure. And the treasure itself? It takes the playful children to get to it. I am not sure about my dream. It will interpret itself in time. Perhaps it is linked to the seminar, or to the physical location of Esalen.

The dream has possible connections to Esalen. Esalen is located in Big Sur, California, which was originally Native American territory. Recently, one of the spiritual fathers of Esalen, Dick Price, had died. The Esalen community was still mourning his loss at this time.

Did any of you dream anything last night?

DAVID: I was amazed that I dreamed anything at all! It's very rare for me to dream. Not only did I dream, but there was a lot of motion in the dream. There was an earthquake and it was so strong I really believed we were having an earthquake. After it was over, nobody else knew it had happened because it was so quiet.

It's interesting because in the meditations we did yesterday, in every channel the same message kept coming up: "Make a major shift!" Whether I was working on something physically, or with an image or dream, the same message came up in all the channels. It kept saying, "Make a major shift." In the dream it was such a powerful earthquake, and afterwards it was all quiet.

ARNY: Mmm. So your meditation, too, tapped into your dreaming body. Just make the shift yourself, like a dragon moving under the earth.

LIZ: I had a dream last night too. In my dream I was first packing my bags and then I was unpacking because I had arrived where I was going. I looked out the window in the dream and saw I was in Jerusalem! I had three Israeli babysitters and I was trying to put up a rail for the crib. I was doing the typical things I do in my life but I was in Jerusalem!

ARNY: You're in Jerusalem? How do you like it?

LIZ: Jerusalem is wonderful. It's strange and complex. It's been the center of so much for so many centuries.

ARNY: Welcome home! Welcome to this old, conflicted religious center. Did anybody else dream something?

Annie, the woman who worked the night before on her diabetes, speaks up.

ANNIE: I had a dream that I was driving my van. I needed to cross a river and I wondered whether or not I should drive the van onto the ferry. I begin to drive the van onto the ferry, but I'm afraid to get on the boat. I go back and as it is pulling out I take a giant leap and jump across onto the ferryboat. There is a sinister man who is the ferryboat driver and he is walking over to me and I don't know quite what the next step is.

ARNY: Say hello!

Annie laughs.

Have it out with him on his ferryboat!

ANNIE: Well, he seems like he could be evil or dangerous. He could kill me. I don't know, but I think if I get across the river it will be good. I feel I'm leaving an old place.

ARNY: Again and again throughout life we are working on the childhood dream, our personal myth. At first the evil one just terrifies us, then it threatens our existence in the form of chronic symptoms and, later, as we join it, it becomes a mysterious ally, which gives us the impetus to live.

Double Signals

Changing to the theme of the morning, Arny begins to introduce relationship work.

I thought of working with relationships this morning. This is another aspect of process work. It's a way of unraveling the dreams and body experiences and discovering their "systemic value," the way they enrich and confound relationships. Almost all relationships are made difficult because you are unaware of the fact that you are dreaming while you are talking.

That dreaming appears in "double" signals. You know, there are many signals which you intend to send. They belong to your primary process. And then there are lots of unintentional signals which you communicate. These signals are in your vocal tone, the way you use your body, your posture, the distance you assume when in communication with others. These unintentional signals we call "double" signals.

The information in these signals is unintended. You do not identify with it. Thus, these signals are like your dreams. They confuse the other person. That is why others sometimes accuse you of doing something that you are not even aware of. You get upset and tell them they are crazy and they say you are a liar. We all know what it is like to get into relationship difficulties. What is the worst relationship problem?

Theresa says jealousy is her biggest problem.

OK. Let's work on that for a moment. Let's see how double signals can help us with jealousy. Should I pretend that I am jealous of you or that you are jealous of me?

THERESA: Let's say that you are always jealous because I am involved with somebody else.

ARNY: Will you play this out with me? Let's say I am jealous of your relationship to the woman next to you. My most common tendency is to repress jealousy. Let's just gossip for a minute. So I ask, "Did you have a nice evening last night with your other friend?"

THERESA: Yeah, a nice time.

ARNY: Well, I'm really happy for you. [*Arny grits his teeth as he says this, and the group laughs. He continues to demonstrate what it looks like to double-signal jealousy.*] Should we have breakfast now? [*He looks away as he asks her.*]

THERESA: Sure.

ARNY: Did you get home on time last night?

THERESA: Well, I was a little late. I decided to stay out a little later.

ARNY: Really! OK. Let's have some breakfast. [*To the group*] Now, if you are looking at me closely you'll see me doing more than just talking to her. I'm acting cool and unaffected, but I'm also

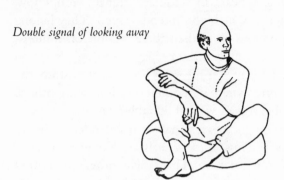

Double signal of looking away

double-signaling. [*He twists his hands as he talks and a participant points to Arny's hands.*]

Well, I hadn't noticed my hands actually! [*Group laughter*] I was focusing on my face! How could you help me with what I'm doing with my hands? Help me get into contact with this hand signal without interpreting it.

A participant says he would ask Arny what his hands are doing.

Most people here in this seminar would give you good feedback if you ask them, "What are you doing with your hands?" But the normal population will not. How else could you work with my hands?

GARY: Mirror them back.

ARNY: OK. That would be good with someone who is not shy. But let's say I am the most difficult client. What would help me then? It might be useful if you were to guess incorrectly but gently into the meaning of my signal. You might say, "I don't understand hands, but yours look like they are relaxing." I would react warmly to that!

Remember, interventions in relationship work must be done in a related fashion. You have to relate to, and support, the person's primary process. You can't expect people to just go directly into the double signals they're making. Shy people need verbal interventions. Clients who are not body shy, however, can work directly and physically with double signals. In such a case, you can ask the person to amplify the hand motion, or you can put one of your hands on one of hers and physically encourage the motions.

Do you see what I'm doing with my hands? I'm stroking them. Now, when I amplify their motion, one hand seems to feel hurt and the other is being nice to it. The idea is that what I'm doing in my double signals is information that I need to bring to awareness, in this case, into the relationship I'm involved in. So if I bring this into relationship I would have to say to my partner across the room "Oh... please be nice to me. I need to know that you love me." You see, the hands are doing this because I am acting like a cool and unaffected person, trying to be open, enlightened, and not jealous. So, my hurt and jealousy is expressed in signals that I do not identify with, like my hands, or in my dreams.

Working gently with double signals relieves the situation. Some jealous people might have the kind of process I do, asking to be loved, while others might be double-signaling anger, with fists or gritted teeth, for example. Each secondary process shows itself as an ongoing series of evolving, transforming signals, and each signal is the right one for a given moment. Finding and bringing in these signals creates rich, deep relationships because it brings in the human, genuine side of people.

[*Arny turns to another participant, Shelly, and asks her to help him demonstrate more about signals.*] Let's say we are in a fight, Shelly. What can we fight about?

SHELLY [*Quickly*]: Money!

ARNY: Aha! Money! OK, let's fight about money for a couple of minutes. How much did that thing cost?

SHELLY: Eleven dollars.

ARNY: Eleven dollars? Where did all that come from?

SHELLY: It's my eleven dollars.

ARNY: What do you mean *your* eleven dollars? All the money that I make goes into the pot. It's ours!

SHELLY: Well, no, this money is for me.

ARNY [*To the group*]: What do you see me doing while I'm looking at Shelly? [*Arny has been sitting straight up, with his legs crossed
and his head held high.*]

Since double signals are incomplete processes, states which
are frozen and cycling, you cannot completely understand
them. We are always in danger of projecting all sorts of wrong
stuff onto them. We forever interpret each other's double signals, usually projecting our own material into them.

Your projections could be correct, but it is always best for
the other if she can discover and communicate the meaning of
her own signals. This particular postural signal, sitting up
straight, means for me... [*Arny pauses, closes his eyes and amplifies his sitting position. He is taking a moment to find out what he is
doing in that posture.*]

Let's see. If I were to put words to this posture that
expressed what I was doing, I would say "I am a really important person and need to be appreciated. And this has nothing
to do with money!"

SHELLY: I am aware when you say that, that I, too, changed my
posture and sat up straighter.

ARNY: What's the difference for you between sitting up straight
and slouching over?

SHELLY: Well, I think sitting up is a stronger position. I feel like
I'm going to need it.

ARNY: So you need a lot of strength. It's important for you to be
powerful and you need encouragement to do that. So on the
surface we're acting like two people having a nice discussion,
but really, underneath, you need to be strong and I need to be
appreciated. If we don't pay attention to our signals, we do
double talk. We speak about one thing while something else is
going on.

JIM: Arny, when you get down to discussing the real issue, what
happens then?

ARNY: I cannot say what will happen when you begin getting
down to what's really going on. But I do know that you then
become congruent. You are more whole, your partner is more
whole, and the relationship itself is more complete. It's a very

magical and unpredictable moment. Your relationship is free to evolve into whatever is trying to happen between you and your partner. In our situation now we will not just talk about money, but about who we both are as people, and the meaning and electricity of our relationship.

THERESA: So with jealousy, for example, if we talk about the fact that you didn't like what I did, that's still not the underlying issue.

ARNY: Is there ever one underlying issue? The issue is only half of it. The other part is, "I want you to be nice to me, please. Do you really like me?" If I really bring that out, the jealousy or relationship issue may be done in a couple of minutes or may even become insignificant. Jealousy and money are just names, and underneath them are processes wanting to be lived more fully.

The problem is not only what she was doing last night. I am deeply involved with whether she loves me. It is very strange and hard to believe unless you've been down to this deeper level once. Once you get down to the deeper feelings below the surface, it relieves things immensely. It's like body-work. You start off with a symptom and before you know it you are in the midst of a drive for completeness.

SUE: Do you need an agreement between the people about how to work with the relationship?

ARNY: It's useful to have an agreement, but not necessary. Who can agree about anything when you're in a battle? If your partner is not interested, you can still work by yourself with your own double signals. You can be working with a blithering idiot, which is often how we feel when we are working on relationship stuff anyhow! The main thing is that we discover ourselves. Once you do this yourself, you feel you have won. You've gotten everything you need and, chances are, the other person will want to win and discover as well.

I'd like to mention different kinds of signals that occur in relationships and then I'd like to work with two people. One common double signal can be seen in posturing, like I just showed you. You can work with how someone is sitting. Are they sitting straight up, leaning back on their arms, lying down or turned away?

Another double signal is movement of the hands and feet which is incongruent with whatever is being said. Perhaps I'm twisting my hands together, or tapping my feet, or stroking my beard. Check out to see whether these movements correspond to what the people are saying. And another really important signal is the distance and angle between us. [*Arny stands up to demonstrate this with Amy. He stands, facing Amy, about eight feet away from her.*]

Let's say Amy and I are going to work on something together and I unconsciously choose this distance from which to communicate. This distance is a lot different than this kind of distance. [*He walks up very close, and stands almost nose to nose with her.*]

So how could you work with the distance between us?

GREG: You can ask the couple if they are aware of it. If they are far apart, you could get them to move even further away and ask them what's right about that.

ARNY: That's right. [*He backs up.*] The way I am now standing feels like I am at an edge. I'm scared or shy about something. I'd like to leave the conversation and drop it, but I can't. How could you work with people who are standing very close? A

Relationship distances

lot of people will go for hours and hours in really close contact without bringing it into their relationship.

    [*Amy and Arny sit very close and face each other.*] What about this distance? How could you work with that?

A participant suggests pushing the couple closer together.

    Yes, gently pushing them closer together. We are now at an edge to get even closer and have a lot of physical contact. [*Arny pauses, and starts to think aloud to himself.*] Let's see, posturing, distance and faces. What else is important? [*To the group*] Watch my face and see what happens. [*Amy and Arny stand about two feet apart and face each other. To Amy*] Tell me I'm a bad swimmer.

AMY: You are an awful swimmer.

ARNY: I am not an awful swimmer!

AMY: But you are. You don't put your arms in right.

Arny pauses and then turns to the group.

ARNY: What do you notice about the color of my eyes?

Everyone laughs, not expecting to have seen such a subtle signal.

    I am trying to demonstrate a strange and important signal, a change of color around the eyes. It's subtle, but important.

    [*To Amy*] Say something really bad.

AMY: You're a lousy runner.

ARNY: I'm not a bad runner.

AMY: Yes you are.

Arny concentrates on changing the coloration around his eyes. He points to the area around his eyes, his cheeks and his ears.

ARNY: Is there discoloration around this part of my face? It's hard to produce.

LISA: Is it a clouding over?

ARNY: Yes, a clouding over. It's a discoloration of the whole area. The color around the eyes changes.

VIVIAN: Not the eyes themselves?

ARNY: The eyes themselves can get cloudy and change. The pupils may widen, too. But it's the area around the eyes and upper cheeks that's really important. The darkening is usually a feeling that someone is having that they don't want to bring in. Sadness or crying.

Try not interpreting double signals, but experiment with a gentle approach. In working with the facial coloration, you might try, "I'm seeing something in your face, but I don't know what it is." This is a blank access statement and is extremely helpful. You leave the content blank so that the people themselves can fill it in. You could ask someone to amplify it, saying, "Could you produce it more?" In this case, most people will say, "Well, what I didn't want to say is that I am feeling sad."

Another way of dealing with double signals, like biting your lip, is to misinterpret them. Let's say Amy and I are talking and I say to her, "Amy, I just know that you have no fears about public performances."

Amy giggles and begins to bite her lip.

Now, she's biting her lip ever so slightly. A useful way of working with a double signal like this is to purposefully misinterpret it. I might say, for example, "Biting your lip means that you're enjoying our discussion, right?"

AMY [*Shakes her head*]: No!

ARNY: So what does your lip mean?

AMY: I'm terrified, scared.

ARNY: Yeah. A purposeful misinterpretation done with humor allows the other person to express more clearly and rapidly what is happening.

MARTHA: Do you do double-signal work in relationship with each other or do you work on your stuff alone?

ARNY: There is no difference. In the older paradigms you did your thing and I did mine, and it was up to heaven to connect and separate us. Now, working on yourself when you are with another person is working on the relationship, because when you are together there is one field and as many sets of double signals as there are people. It's easier to see a field rather than two separate individuals, as you'll see in just a minute.

*Introversion as
a double signal*

My most typical double signal happens when I meet someone for the first time. I'll meet somebody and show you. [*Arny asks Amy to help him demonstrate. They stand up and act as if they are meeting for the first time. Arny shakes hands with Amy.*] Hello. It's nice to meet you. [*As he speaks, he drops his head slightly and turns away.*]

If it's so nice to see you, why am I looking at the floor? I am saying to Amy that it is nice to see her, and I'm saying indirectly that while I meet her I must look down to stay centered in myself. Since I am not always able to express this signal, I sometimes confuse people. What happens then is interesting. One set of double signals creates another set. I double-signal and then whomever I'm meeting picks it up and acts strangely. Often, they'll start to talk about something I have no idea about: "Do you remember me? I saw you ten years ago in Mexico." or something like that. Then I get upset and think, "Don't you notice where I am?"

When you work with relationship stuff, who did what to whom ceases to be important. Causality is not a useful concept in relationship. We really do not know who did what first. Perhaps I look down because the other person is also doing something strange. Causal thinking and causal approaches cannot help us with relationships. More important than causality is awareness.

Thus the common statement, "If it weren't for you, I wouldn't do this!" is a causal way of thinking. Of course we all feel this way at times, especially when we're in the midst of a tense and difficult field. But it is impossible to objectively say any one person is the cause of anything.

Double Edges

One more theoretical point. Most relationships are not satisfactory unless we can work through the double-edge system, the edges both partners have on each side of the relationship. Let me explain what I mean.

[*Amy turns to one of the participants sitting nearby.*] Let's say you and I are working together and Amy is our facilitator. Amy notices that each of us has an edge. We both have edges; this phenomenon is what I call the double edge. I have an edge to express something and you have an edge to express something, too. What will Amy do?

Normally, she'd take sides and go with whomever she liked best. Today, however, for the purpose of our training, she's going to take both sides, first yours and then mine. The facilitator must flow like a river and can take one side after the other, helping both people with their awareness, their double signals and the edges they have to expressing certain things. By siding with awareness, and not with any one person, she maintains a fluid neutrality.

However, in relationship work it is impossible to remain neutral, unless you fake neutrality and act like a computer. One way to use your tendency to take sides is to go ahead and take someone's side, and then switch and take the other person's side too. You will almost always find that you first take the side of the one who needs the most help at that moment. It is then your job to help the one with whom you are siding to notice what she cannot express and help her to express herself. Or help her to notice what the other is signaling.

When you're working with a relationship, notice with whom you side. Go over to that person's side and help her go over the edge and express what she feels herself. Then switch sides and help the other person. You'll notice yourself switching automatically. All sides are weak in relationship work. All of us lose our awareness as we fall into the altered states created by strong emotions.

A Relationship Experiment

OK. That's enough theory. Would two people like to do this in front of the group? It's a little embarrassing, but it could be a lot of fun.

A man and a woman volunteer to work. As they come into the middle of the room, Arny asks "Do you two know each other?" They both say no. "That's wonderful," Arny says. "Let's work together and then everyone will have a chance to try it in groups of three." The man and woman walk to the middle of the room and stand about four feet apart.

WOMAN [*Turns to the man*]: I don't know your name.
MAN: My name's Eric. [*A different Eric than in Chapter 3.*]
WOMAN: Mine's Fran.

They both say "hi" to each other.

ARNY [*To the group*]: They're doing great, aren't they?

Fran, Eric, and the group all giggle. Fran and Eric talk for a few minutes. The situation is a bit awkward. It's difficult to hear what they are saying, but we catch snatches of the conversation. They're discussing what they do for a living, their children, and where they live.

ERIC: So, you live in Seattle?

Fran nods. Eric asks her if she would like to sit down. She says yes and, as they start to sit down, she rubs her chest. Arny walks towards them.

ARNY: Well, just before you sit down, there was something wonderful happening there. Would you mind standing up again for a minute?

Fran and Eric stand up. Arny turns to Fran and, using his hands, he shows her what her posture was while she was talking to Eric. He sculpts her body in the direction it was going while she was

Fran and Eric

talking to Eric. He pulls her left shoulder back slightly, but keeps her head still turned toward Eric.

ARNY [*To Fran*]: I want to exaggerate it. Please excuse me.

Fran pulls her shoulders further back.

> Yes, that's it. That's beautiful. This is what you were doing, though I have no idea what that signal is.

FRAN: Well, my feet are pointed in one direction, my body in another and my face is pointing in another direction!

ARNY [*Touching Fran's shoulder*]: Well, let's just work on this area. Let's pretend that this posture is great. It's just what you need. We just don't know what it is. It's beautiful. [*Arny mirrors Fran's posture, the tilt of her head and the pulled-back shoulders.*]

FRAN [*Looking at Arny as he mirrors her posture*]: Well, that looks very defensive. When I look at you I think, "Gee, he's trying to defend himself."

ARNY: Well, let's pretend that your defending yourself is an intelligent thing to do. It's smart. What do you need to defend yourself against?

FRAN: It's hard for me when people ask me what I do. I don't like identifying with my job. I'm happier when I can focus on just being. But I feel a little guilty about it.

ARNY: Yeah, now just go on with Eric in any way you want.

FRAN [*Turns to Eric*]: That's what happens to me when people ask me what I'm doing.

Hearing this, Eric appears to awaken.

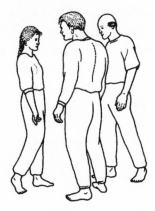

Tilted head and shoul-
ders pulled back

ERIC: I feel an inability to communicate what's really going on in me.

Arny now goes over to Eric.

ARNY: There's also something you're doing. Can I come to your side a minute?

Eric nods.

> I want you to feel that whatever you're doing is a good thing. You're not just shy or embarrassed. I'll show you one of the things that you are doing, just a tiny bit. [*Arny helps him exaggerate his posture by pushing his shoulders forward a bit more than they were and depressing his chest a little bit further, since it was*

Working with Eric

slightly depressed when he was talking to Fran.] Hold that until you know what it's trying to say. What is the difference between the posture we just amplified and its opposite?

[*Arny now uses his hands to guide Eric into an opposite posture, one in which he stands up straight with his chest sticking out.*]

ERIC: I don't know. The first way is like protecting my heart. Being too exposed.

ARNY: No kidding. Tell her about that heart. Tell her how you need to protect it. And you, Fran, you tell him more about what it's like to just be. But go ahead, Eric, tell her about your heart.

ERIC [*To Fran*]: It is very easy for me to get hurt. It's easy for me to get involved with someone and then they go away. So I need to protect my heart. I want to be careful so I don't get hurt. [*Eric continues to protect his heart even more by sitting on the floor, hunching over and crossing his arms over his legs.*]

ARNY: Far out. You're protecting yourself.

Fran looks at Eric and changes from the posture that she had been in.

FRAN: Now you look more protected. It's somehow easier for me to just be, to relax. I can just be.

Eric and Fran seem to have suddenly discovered each other. They give each other a big hug. Arny hugs his pillow, and the group laughs.

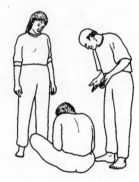

Eric being careful

Arny then turns to the group and encourages everyone to try the same exercise in triads. One person acts as facilitator for the other two and follows the flow of her or his perceptions. If she finds herself tending to be interested in or supporting one member of the couple, then she must practice following her perceptions and take that person's side by assisting with the expression of double signals and encouraging her over an edge. Then after one edge of the double-edge system has been crossed, the facilitator must move to the other side and help the other person express unconscious signals and experiment with edges. In this way the facilitator practices awareness and fluidity.

The group breaks up into groups of three. After about half an hour, they all come back together for a discussion.

Discussion

ARNY: Well, it looks like most of you were able to do that pretty well. Was there anyone who needed help in completing things? Did you make any discoveries?

CHERYL: We had fun.

ARNY: I'd like to tell you something very meditative you can do in order to work on double signals when you're having relationship trouble and you start to cycle. You know, like those all-night conversations, the ones that go on until at least three in the morning! When you've had enough and think it should stop, try this.

Ask your partner to let you go internal for a moment. Go internal, feel what you are feeling, and switch channels. Remember the meditation work we did yesterday morning? This is inner work, but now you integrate your inner work into your relationship work. Make a picture out of what you're feeling and tell your partner about that picture. Then let the picture unravel itself and just ask your partner to observe.

Let me show you how to do it. Perhaps I can do it here while I am with all of you. After all, I am in relationship with you as a group right now. I'm sure I'm double-signaling, like I frequently do. But this time I am going to do it consciously. I am going to go inside.

[*He pauses, looks down and his left hand begins to rise.*] I notice that I'm feeling something. I'm feeling this new thing that's been driving me crazy lately. [*Both hands begin to rise.*] I feel something very quiet. The picture I get from the feeling is a pond that doesn't have any ripples. This is where I am and anything else I would do would only be half congruent for me. And I am in conflict with myself about it.

PAM: What is it?

ARNY [*Quietly*]: It's this feeling I've had now for months and months of being extremely quiet inside. It feels like nothing much is happening in my head. It's just quiet.

Now I want to relate to the picture. If I don't relate to this picture or the feeling inside of me, then they can only come out as double signals and you react to them. Awareness is a way of reducing relationship tension. Let me vocalize my awareness.

I have this particular picture of quiet water and am in conflict with it. I don't want to have it. I want to relate normally to you. Now, this picture of the pond just stays, and I find myself getting closer to it. Oh, this reminds me of my dream of last night, the wise head on the puppet. My body now becomes still as I quiet down and my head clears.

[*After a moment*] With no facilitator I have to be my own relationship advisor. I use my own awareness of proprioception and visualization to work on double signals.

GREG: What would you do in an interaction with somebody on the street who doesn't know about process work or doesn't know anything about psychology, and who would think you were nuts?

ARNY: If the other person became afraid when I went internal, I would respect that and wouldn't reveal my inner world. I would follow my awareness internally and only bring the effects out. It's enough to be responsible for your own awareness and to react. Waking others up is fine, but don't forget it is still a democracy. Let the other be as responsible as she wants to.

PAT: It sounds as if you don't criticize people for the secondary process.

ARNY: How could I? After all, we all dream.

CHAPTER 11

Client Problems and Group Work

This is the last session of the seminar, late Sunday morning. Everyone sits a bit closer, and there is a mood of expectation in the air. Some participants are anxious to ask more questions about working with clients.

MIKE: Arny, I see with a great deal of admiration how dutifully you contain consciousness for both the person you work with and for yourself. Could you speak a little bit about your work with clients who very easily get into experiences, but are not so able to contain them? Does it ever happen that someone gets into their stuff and goes wild?

ARNY: No one I have worked with until now has gone psychotic! Why? I restrain myself from asking people to process parts of themselves which they are not able to use and which they have great edges to. I break the rule, however, if they are in a desperate physical situation or near death. Then I might ask them to go over edges because it is more painful and more dangerous to stay high and safe, quiet and contained.

Awareness is the only container we need. Let me give you an example. Take a person in a manic, desperate state. I'm thinking of somebody who was really wild, somebody who looked like this. By the way, in Portland and Zurich we are in the middle of creating clinics for people in extreme states. The person I'm thinking of looks like this. I'll show you a drama that is not easily contained. [*Arny stands up and walks to the other side of the room.*] Imagine that I'm this man in his thirties who has been in and out of mental institutions for a long time, off and on psychopharmica for years.

[*He walks around in the circle, waving his arms about, and speaking loudly and very rapidly.*] You know, well, they told me when I came here, you know, they did, well, what the hell. I mean, I've been telling you, you know, what happened when I got here. The train stopped and the people, blah blah blah... [*Arny continues gesturing and making noises, indicating a nonstop flow of ideas. He continues at a great speed, getting faster and louder, and waving his arms even more rapidly and violently. Finally he finishes and, like himself again, he walks back to his spot. He turns to the group.*]

Where is the edge in what that man is doing?

None of the participants volunteers an answer. Arny gets up and acts like the manic man again, this time speaking more directly to the group and commenting on his state.

I am crazy. I need lots of meds. Thank God I have these downers! If I didn't have these downers, I would be going like thirty-five times as fast right now. God, I'd be going really fast. But I am really a sick person and I want you to heal me, doctor, and for Godsakes *do it fast!*

[*As himself again*] What's happening there? What is primary?

One participant says that the man identifies himself as being crazy.

Yes. He said, "I'm a sick person." That means he identifies with being sick. It's a primary process. He said, "Doctor, I'm sick. Heal me now!" So he has the identity of a psychiatric patient. He deals with himself as a psychiatrist would, telling himself he is sick and needs medication. Now how would you work with him?

[*Arny stands up and plays the man again. He waves his arms in the air and begins the rapid-fire speech.*]

Yeah, and you know…

STEVE: Slow it down?

ARNY [*Laughing*]: Well, slowing it down is what *you'd* like, but I don't know about the client! But how?

KATHY: Why not tell him to speed up?

ARNY: That would be interesting. How about picking up his secondary process, his incomplete arm movements? [*Arny shows the participants how the arm motions are incomplete. He waves his arms in the air, mutters and slaps his own thighs in an incomprehensible manner.*]

Incomplete movements make no sense and repeat themselves. One of the best ways to complete a motion is to inhibit it. This increases awareness of the movement impulse. When I worked with him in reality, I caught one of his arms in motion as it was coming down. [*Arny comes forward and plays the manic client. Amy demonstrates catching his hand as it comes down.*]

I said to him, "What is going on here?" And the man looked at me and yelled, "I am really… angry!"

I helped him to express his anger, but he didn't know why he was angry. So I said, "Stop talking so much and just hit." He hit the punching bag in my practice a few times. "What are you angry about?" I asked. And he said, "What I am *really* angry about is…" and he started to cry. "What I am really angry about is… that when I was a kid they put me in an

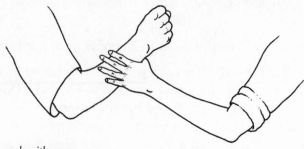

Movement work with anger

orphanage. I went from orphanage to orphanage and I was never wanted."

So I asked, "Are you crazy or are you angry?" And he said, "I didn't realize it, but I am furious, absolutely furious about what happened to me. I was always being put in an orphanage." And then he cried.

Where is he being put in an orphanage now? How is he in an orphanage *now?* He is in an orphanage by calling himself sick. That's not wanting the kid. In other words, the child, his secondary process of anger and fury, is also furious with the primary one, the medical attitude which calls him sick.

Discovering his anger through the movement work slowed him down immediately. So now I can finally answer your question about containment. You do not have to contain people. You don't have to hold them in or push them out. Programs can't really contain people, but the people's own experiences and your awareness are the best containment.

It can even be dangerous to contain processes. It is dangerous to follow only one part of ourselves. With this man, it would be dangerous to follow only the primary side, which wants to cool him down, or only the secondary, cathartic side, his explosiveness. His coolness is provocative; it provokes his anger. By asking him about his anger in the midst of it, I am helping him bring the processes together. The whole process balances itself, and only then is it truly wise and self-contained.

Everyone is silent, and then Melissa speaks up.

MELISSA: One of my clients... Oh, it's very painful, and emotional...

Arny intervenes and asks Melissa to show the client.

ARNY: One of the best things that you can do when talking about a client that you are working with is to give us sensory-grounded information about the situation. In fact, half the solution to problems in practice is recalling the sensory-grounded information. If you don't, the story you tell us from your practice is really about your own psychology. That's fine,

too, but it will not be as useful to you or to the client as recalling the real person. So, could you show her to us?

MELISSA: She's very, very pretty, and... [*Before she completes the
description, she sits up very tall and straight.*]

ARNY: That's it. Act like her. Hello there, what's your name?

MELISSA [*As the client*]: Don't get too close. I don't like to be
touched.

ARNY: No kidding?

He gets up and cautiously starts to come closer. Everyone watches
tensely.

> This is like an open invitation to process the anger there. One
> part wants help, but another part warns you against something
> which you as a human being want to do, indeed must do. So
> in doing it, she will have to get angry, and you will have to
> deal with that.

MELISSA: That's right! She is like her mother. She won't let herself
be seen crying. She turns the chair around so I won't see her.

ARNY: So someone is looking. She's in the middle of a struggle
with some negative critic who is against emotion, against some
part of herself that needs to come out. Perhaps that critic is the
one who makes life impossible for you as a therapist. If she
does not want to discuss or get into that critic, then you will
end up being criticized by the unconscious critic in her and
may have to have a personal confrontation with her about it.

MELISSA: I guess I am afraid to do that.

ARNY: You sound very real. We can all see here what might be
helpful. Even though I can give intelligent suggestions, they
may not necessarily be your process with her. So knowing you
is important, and since you feel safer approaching her verbally,
you must follow your way. That is what process work could
mean for you.

> Perhaps you want to first talk to her. You could say, "Cli-
> ent, dear, please make sure that the action that I do is right for
> you. I would like to try something strong. I want to disobey
> your directions and go more deeply into the contact problem.
> I wonder if you would allow me to try it."

By describing your interventions intellectually ahead of time, she has options and control. If the client doesn't respond with good feedback to what you are doing, regardless of how brilliant it is, it's not the right track for the moment. The right interaction at the wrong time is off.

TERRY: How do you recognize signals that tell you to stop, that tell you that you're not following the process anymore?

ARNY: I do not always know. I don't try to know what signals mean. If I am insecure about someone's signals I ask them. "I am looking at you and you are biting your lip. Is that a negative signal? Should we not be going in this direction?"

Group Work

Let's do a group process to complete what we've been doing this weekend. Should I offer you some group theory? You all know everything in your hearts anyway.

We live in what mathematicians call a field. A field creates the atmosphere and organizes our feelings. It's somewhat like a dream looking for different figures to fill it.

You won't believe this but I have always hated groups. I felt they had no room for the individual. Now I realize that what I hated about them is that they organize and polarize us so that we get tied down to a given role. In any given field there is always the good guy and the bad guy, the savior and the victim, the leader and the follower. These roles are important. They are the dream figures which the group field uses to express itself, but we do not have to get stuck in any one of them forever.

The roles that people are drawn to play in a group are like the poles of a magnet. If there is one role, another always arises to balance it. A field always needs these polarities to create the tension and the atmosphere. Thus where there is a leader with an idea, there must be a group or person with another idea. In other words, every leader is fated to be challenged. The follower either comes forward and expresses herself or she sits back, silently, feeling like an outsider. The leader picks up this tension and starts to feel insecure. It seems as if all these human processes are part of our being parts of one organic whole. Groups have a tendency to create roles and to remain balanced as much as possible. The tension that arises is normal. It presses us towards knowing one another, towards division, unity, and spiritual experience.

We don't have much time today for group theory or processing, but we can touch upon the field in the room just now, before we break up this morning. Does our field have specific parts or is there just a general feeling?

The group suggests different parts that might be in the field. They agree that there are leaders and appreciative followers.

Let's find the roles which may be present and give the group field a form. Let's see if we can fill the roles. I'm going to help fill them myself. Let me go over to this side of the room.

[*He walks to the far side of the circle.*] Let's say that this spot here, where I'm now standing, is a position for the leaders, for anyone feeling identified with leadership. And then there must be a position for the critic. Where is that?

A participant says that the critic's position is on the opposite side of the room. Arny points to a place in the middle, between the leader and the critic position.

OK, let's put a position here for positive feelings. And let's make a position for the silent people, for those not talking. There must be a position for the ones who just feel and observe what's happening.

I'll start by filling some of the positions myself. See if you are also pulled to fill one or more of the positions. We are all so complex that we never fit the roles set up by a group. We have more than the one feeling or thought in us. Our feelings may belong to several roles. We almost never have one single feeling, and we never really want to be in one single role.

The danger of group life is being drawn into a role and held down to its one-sided position. We are all too whole for that. So feel free to take as many roles as you genuinely feel and switch roles whenever you need to.

Now I want to go in the critic position. Amy, could you stand in the leader position?

[*Arny goes to the critic spot and Amy stands in the leader's position. Arny now speaks from the critic's role.*]

OK, it was a good seminar but I was frustrated the whole time by the agenda. I understand you guys were under a contract with Esalen to do an introductory course, but I wanted to be able to go slower, to focus in on one aspect of process work. That's what I would have needed more of.

AMY [*As the leader*]: Good. Any one thing you would have liked to focus on?

ARNY: For some reason I would like you to focus on serious illnesses or relationships. [*Arny now walks over to the spot for positive feelings, and says to Amy, who is still in the leader's role*] I liked you. You were basically OK.

[*He walks to the quiet spot and stands there quietly. After a minute or so, he goes back over to the leader's role, next to Amy.*] That was a short seminar. Ten hours is brief. If anyone would like to take any of these positions, please just step into them.

Wendy walks over to the positive spot.

WENDY: I have something for the positive position. I came here thinking I was going to have just a weekend by the ocean. I also wanted to familiarize myself with your work because so many of my friends have talked about it. I didn't know I was going to go so deeply into my own process and I am very appreciative of that. I was able to do something very important

The leaders
✗

Silence ✗   ✗ Positive feelings

✗

The critic

Roles in the group field

in my relationship with my husband and I feel great. Thank you.

I had a quick thought this morning that when we go back home I'd like to start a production company or something that brings this kind of event, so you'll be hearing from me about that.

She goes to the silent spot, makes a quiet humming sound and then sits down again. Others come up and stand in the positive spot and praise the seminar, the work and the experiences they had. Steve stands up and goes over to the critic's role.

STEVE [*Hesitantly*]: Well, I felt a sort of frustration about... well, what about all the other parts? I have the feeling that my questions did not quite get to the heart. I didn't get a sense of where it all fits in.

ARNY [*In the leader's role*]: "Other parts" of what? Right now your questions aren't getting to the heart of things. I don't understand what you're saying. Say more.

STEVE: I've been trying to make my questions more concise but I couldn't quite.

ARNY: Well, thank you. That's helpful. Maybe I can wait longer in the future and help to draw you and others out. Maybe now?

STEVE: Yes, this seems like a group of professionals. What about people who just wander in, not knowing anything about techniques? This work is so powerful that people will often end up in very sensitive areas. I guess my question is a concern about what happens to these crucial experiences after we all leave here.

ARNY: I need your help with this. My first impulse is to get around that question by saying that these seminars are mainly educational, not therapeutic. I try to get people to take responsibility for themselves. But that's not the whole truth. I also want to take care of everyone, even if I say I don't.

I do tell people to connect with other seminar participants or facilitators outside the workshop to work through unfinished stuff. But I have to admit, I can't care for everyone, even though I want to. So I'm not as responsible as I could be in this regard, but, on the other hand, I am not a god and do like spending time away from everyone, in meditation, alone too.

But I'm not satisfied with my answers. Let me come over to your side. [*He goes over to the critic's role and stands next to Steve.*] Now I am with you in your spot. I want to say to the leader, "Well, good enough, but every public person has responsibility for those she or he touches!"

[*Arny goes back over to leader's role. He pauses for a minute, then attempts to answer the criticism. He starts to speak, then stops.*] Well, uhm, I think I'm at an edge. What I want to say is that I do take responsibility! I feel very, very concerned about you here and about the world situation. That's why I'm traveling so much and working in difficult places and Third World areas where it is tough! I know I need to develop cross-cultural methods and the only way to do that is to learn from the world itself. Most of all, I can hardly sleep at night if I think that what I'm doing is incomplete, too painful, too long, too limited, or if it creates the wrong feeling atmosphere.

But I am not only a therapist. I am a normal person, a teacher and I am also interested in the fate of all of us. For me, a seminar is only indirectly therapeutic; it is a type of training, not only in psychology, but in living. I am attached to this work, because I like it but also because something unknown is asking me to take part in the overall transformation and awakening which we are all part of.

Steve walks over to the positive spot.

STEVE: Well, thanks. That touches me. I also feel the breadth of the work and how it touches the individual.

Now another participant, Joan, walks over to the positive spot and turns to Arny.

JOAN: Arny, I loved your energy and humor. Now I want to go to the leader position myself.

[*She walks over to the leader role, and Arny moves to the positive role. As he walks away, she speaks to him.*] Wait. I want you to stay here with me.

ARNY: I'm coming back there in a minute, but I want to tell you from the positive spot that I think you could be a fantastic leader. I hear it in your voice and the way that you stand.

JOAN: This is a big place for me to stand in. [*She moves over to the positive role, and turns to the group.*] Thanks to all of the people who helped me get here, all my friends this morning, and you, Arny. [*She embraces Arny.*] I want more information about your Oregon and Swiss training programs so I can come. That's probably the scariest thing that I have ever said.

Cheryl marches out into the positive role. She turns to Arny.

CHERYL: You're not as crazy as I thought. That's what I've learned this weekend. I learned how to de-dramatize things and to use humor. The child quality in you lifts me out of my serious, analytic perspective. I appreciate that immensely. I also did a lot of work on myself yesterday and this morning and it was a wonderful opportunity.

LARRY: I love your crazy wisdom. You're much crazier than I thought and I love it.

ARNY [*To Larry*]: Yeah, you're a crazy maniac, too! Craziness and clowning allow us to enjoy our transitions!

RACHEL [*In the silent position*]: Some of you I haven't met in form as much as in spirit—there are so many of you. Being here with you, Arny and Amy, made me feel so creative.

[*She goes to the leader spot.*] I want to walk up here because that's what I'm learning now, [*Beginning to cry*] to follow my own power and my path. I've been coming here all my life to be who I am and to let myself be seen, and I have to take that out into the world now. You're going to see more of me.

The group claps as Rachel finishes speaking.

MARIA: I'm very introverted, so it's pretty hard for me to stand in the positive role. I came here basically because I got a very nice letter from Amy. I had written to her in Zurich, so I was predisposed to like her.

[*To Arny*] I wanted to meet you because I'd heard so many different things about you and many sounded too good to be true. "Arny said this," and "Arny's wonderful," and so on, and I thought, "Come on. Arny's like everyone else."

And then I had a dream about a week ago which I didn't understand because the figure in the dream looked very much like you. But at the time I didn't know that. I came to the workshop and have appreciated you both, your accessibility, honesty, and the fact that you and Amy continue to work on yourselves.

Many charismatic people make dramatic things happen, but it somehow hasn't set well with me. Yet what I've seen you do is genuine. It comes from who you are.

GARY [*In the critical position*]: I don't have a criticism. I have a question. Do you ever get scared? It seems to me there's some strong physical stuff coming at you, especially from men that are twice the size of you. How do you evaluate how far you can go and how do you protect yourself?

ARNY: Where I grew up you had to fight to get along. So I don't get afraid much of physical contact. I protect myself by staying very close to the ground. I don't know any martial arts stuff. But I have learned a great deal by studying video recordings of my work.

After having worked with all kinds of wild people, even murderers, I discovered something. Until now I have never come across a situation where aggression, when processed with awareness, has not flowed into something very useful for all. Awareness must be the best home for almost anything to develop.

However, if I do get scared, then I say it or use it. I run away. I tell people I'm scared of them. I'll admire someone else's strength. Sometimes the safest thing to do is to be scared! Being afraid is a reaction that belongs in the process, too!

But working with anger in movement is not everybody's cup of tea. There are many ways to process things. If you are afraid of someone who is angry, then, once they're in touch with it, ask them to stop moving and visualize it or hit a pillow or make angry sounds. That is the business of channel changing. Remember, if someone chooses you to work with, then it is your particular nature, including your fears, inabilities, and tendencies that he or she needs, not mine or anyone else's.

GARY: Thanks. Did you consciously have your knee up when you fought last night with Ron, the big ape?

ARNY: Yes.

GARY: I thought so.

RON: I let him put his knee there so he wouldn't get hurt!

ARNY [*Laughing*]: That verifies the feeling I have about Ron. He has a big heart.

TESS [*Standing in the positive place*]: I felt utter gentleness from both of you.

ARNY: Amy's sweeter than I am.

Laughter.

TESS: I'm used to working hard, but I can't figure out whether you do, because you work so gently.

ARNY: Sometimes I feel that there is nothing to do. I actually feel sometimes like I'm on vacation when I work.

TESS: Thank you. [*She hugs Arny.*]

ARNY: There must be a place for the spirit someplace. I felt it when I was hugging you just now. Let's make a spot for the spirit over here. [*Arny walks over to the right.*]

Danny moves over to the role of the spirit.

DANNY: I learned a great deal from you, Arny, how to honor people. And I find that to be the solution to the global situation that is going on. You really bow down to people and I admire

The spirit in the field group

that a lot. [*He now moves to the critic's role.*] And I did feel a little frustrated with the short introductory bits and pieces. But at least I'll know what I want the next time I go to a workshop. I'd like to do more work on relationships.

ARNY: I promise!

RON: I'm quite nervous. I've been active and have worked here at Esalen for a while. There are very few people I've met who strike me as profound. I don't know if that is the right word, and I don't know who you really are. How could you have made this profound impact? And yet you have. It's been quite a privilege to be in your workshop.

I think what I want to say is that Esalen needs people like you. It's going through a point of transition, which most people don't know about. Esalen needs powerful people, knowledgeable people, people who are able to communicate and teach what they know, and teach what comes from this spot, the spirit. And that's how you strike me.

As soon as you made a spot for the spirit, I understood your impact on me. I hope you come back and it would be wonderful if you would do more work here. And it's because I'm tied to Esalen. Esalen exposed me to things that I never had exposure to before. I have a real commitment to Esalen as an institution even though there are other places that are great as well.

ARNY: Something in me almost starts to cry when you say that, but I don't know what it is. Thanks. I'm very touched by what you said.

RON: Normally I occupy the critic's spot over there.

ARNY [*Immediately*]: Really? Do it if you need to.

RON [*Smiles*]: It's a pleasure to be in the positive role! [*He walks over to Arny and they embrace. Then Ron steps back and looks at Arny.*] I want to pick you up! [*He lifts Arny off the floor, in a way reminiscent of his work the night before.*]

Everyone laughs and applauds.

CATHERINE: I come from the Third World myself. And your idea that sickness has the key, that's shamanism. [*Now speaking in the*

critic's role] And I'm pissed off you're in Zurich! You're so far
away. I hope you come here more, to the West Coast.

ARNY: We will. We're moving to Portland and will be living on
the Oregon coast.

Janet moves to the role of the silent one and breaks out into dance,
raising her arms over her head and then leaping from the floor.

JANET: I really love the elf that you are and it takes one to know
one. [*She runs to Arny as everyone laughs. She jumps into his arms.
He catches her in the air. Then she moves back to the place for the
spirit and lowers her head.*] Thank you so much.

AMY [*In the spirit role*]: I feel so emotional it's hard for me to talk.
It's usually very hard for me to be in groups of people. This
shyness, too, must be a role which the group needs.

   Last year when we came to Esalen I felt uncomfortable a
lot. This year I felt very warmly received, and this group feels
special to me. The thing that touches me the most, I guess, is
this spirit, the power of your processes which appeared here.
All of us are working towards a similar goal and for me to feel
that in a group of this size is relieving.

   It's hard to leave the feeling of hope and helpfulness we've
created here together. And, Arny, I feel it is an honor to be
with you, to see you teach and to see the effect that you have
on people. It touches me and is just wonderful to see.

Handstand of the new leader

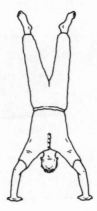

She begins to move back to her seat. Arny pauses. He shuffles a bit shyly, not quite knowing how to deal with her.

ARNY: Hmm, Amy, before you go back... wait. You always surprise me. I am speechless. You make me shy... You are my teacher in loving.

They hug briefly. Both are shy and Amy sits down. Everyone now seems shy. Gary breaks the silence by laughing happily.

GARY: The lightness here makes me think about a new type of leadership. [*He walks over to the leader's spot and jumps into a handstand! People clap and laugh. Gary speaks from his upside down position.*] The new leadership is playful, not authoritative. It's not the kind of leadership we've been used to in the past, because, I think, it's connected to the spirit spot.

People become silent as the group process and the workshop complete themselves. They spontaneously and quietly join hands with one another to create a circle. They sit silently for a minute, mostly with heads down, some quietly and some whispering to each other. After a few minutes, they stand up and begin to say their good-byes.

CHAPTER 12

Working in the Hot Tub

A few months after the seminar we were invited back to Esalen again, this time not merely into the hot tubs for a weekend, but into the heat of Esalen's own individual process. We were invited to be resident trainers at Esalen for five weeks to work with the entire community.

What a job! We entered a complex extended community of almost two hundred people still mourning the death of Dick Price, their former leader, and experiencing the resulting fragmentation into conflicting factions. Esalen presented us with more than enough opportunities to test our methods of conflict resolution and community creation. Having forged our tools in the fires of racism in Africa, tensions in the Middle East, and group processes in Europe and the United States, we wondered if they were suitable or sufficient for what we would encounter at Esalen. We wondered what we would be learning in the little world of Big Sur; would living inside the organization we worked for change our theories or practice? In many ways this group seemed to be like other groups and organizations, where the workers and teachers strained against the system for more contact and influence on the management, and where all feared the dissolution of their world.

But Esalen is not like other organizations we have worked for. Though it naturally reflected characteristics of all institutions, it has managed to maintain a spirit of adventure and an openness towards change. How did it do this? To answer this, we must ask another question. What is Esalen?

Born from the experimental fires and transformation of the Sixties, Esalen was the *enfant terrible* that created an environment that enabled Fritz Perls and Gestalt therapy, Ida Rolf and Rolfing, Will Schutz and his encounter method, and many other humanistic approaches and schools to grow and develop. It housed Gregory Bateson, Stan Grof, Ram Dass, Joseph Campbell, Alexander Lowen, and many others.

Today, in the Nineties, Esalen is like a youth slipping into adulthood. Still the first and foremost of its kind in the Western world, it is primarily a conference and retreat center presenting new or popular psychological traditions, and esoteric teachers and thinkers on the cutting edges of science and the humanities. According to Michael Murphy, one of Esalen's leaders, the place is "...less dominated by the metaphor of therapy and more by the arts, contemplation, intellectual inquiry, and social outreach." *(Los Angeles Times Magazine,* Dec. 6, 1987). Yet Esalen still radiates an atmosphere of mystery, exploration, and inner growth.

Esalen, like any other community, cannot really be understood from the outside. Our first experience of its beautiful surroundings was tempered by the tense atmosphere in which many personal interactions were embedded. This isolated little world, its nearest neighbor one and a half hours to the north, seemed to be simmering in its own troubled juices. As we made friends and slipped into the family, we sympathized with, and, in fact, were infected by, its problems.

Dick Price, one of the founders of Esalen and a confirmed outdoors man, had recently died while hiking in the mountains near Esalen. He was apparently meditating in a sitting position as a large rock fell on him from the mountain peak above. His soft-spoken way, gentle approach to Gestalt therapy, and his retiring manner had been crucial in keeping Esalen together.

But just as important as Dick's legend was the eternal and permeating spirit of the rough, dry land. This property created a belief in, and love for, the physical environment, which one can only experience directly. We felt the power of the Native Americans and of the land, and trusted that whatever happened to the political entity of Esalen, the work on that land could not fail as long as the hot sulfur springs continued to run.

The story of Esalen's transformation actually gives hope to a larger world riddled with pain and symptoms. The problems in inner cities, in the Middle East, in Africa, and in other Third World countries, are found in every community. Most of all, groups are terrified by their own fragmentation. What we learned at Esalen was that radical and innovative change may be possible in the shortest imaginable period of time.

The Beginning Violence of Encounter

Our first job was to pull ourselves together. Luckily, I remembered lessons I had learned elsewhere. The feelings we have as facilitators are often dreamed up by unrepresented parts of the group. At various times we were joyful, afraid, homesick, and even belligerent. We frequently found ourselves feeling oversensitive, in part because the community itself was not able to contact its own sensitivity. We were constantly confronted by the questions, "Who are we and who are they?" and we failed to answer them.

The entire community process there was unforgettable. The first tense large meeting was held in Huxley. Everyone was invited. We started by forming a huge circle, feeling the atmosphere and trying to sense the roles present in the group field. We located the roles of spiritual believers, rebels, those seeking comfort, the management, and the busy workers of Esalen.

We barely had time to explain the concepts of edges and tensions when those who felt connected to the rebel role grabbed the chance to finally express themselves. They broke out with surprising vehemence against the management role. Those who were in the other roles—the spiritual center, comfort seekers and even the busy workers—scattered and slipped away as the rebel faction

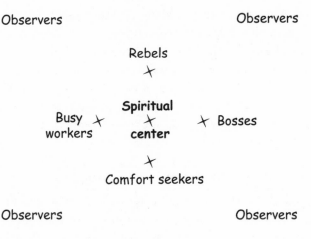

Esalen field roles during the first group process

blasted away at the management, leaving only those two positions on the floor of our global process theater.

The content of the rebels' fury was important, but paled against their anger. The radical violence of the encounter period of the Sixties that we witnessed that evening seemed to be the last stand of a cathartic breakthrough paradigm. It is one state in a larger process, a rough form of communication, shared mainly by those who feel their messages are unheard.

Amy and I cowered in the corners as the pent-up powers of Esalen raged at one another across the room. We, too, came close to getting in the line of fire when we were momentarily accused of supporting one side against the other. OUCH! We had ample opportunity to practice our innerwork methods while we withdrew for a few moments to the corner, away from the aggressive storm. Amy sensed the tensions even more than I and was almost ill during these beginning sessions.

As the management role fought back, members of the community adopted the conflict resolution methods we had offered of switching roles and experiencing the other side. Individuals used their awareness to sense which role they were feeling, and then went into these roles and expressed themselves. The rebel-critics slowly transformed and began to model the changes they were asking for. They succeeded in bringing the conflict to a momentary resolution after two hours of fighting.

The local earth spirits must have been pleased, for as the group processes ended, rain poured down upon Esalen, ending an apparent two-year drought in that area of northern California. Was this an "accident" or does the synchronicity between the rain and the group process resolution indicate a connection between the human atmosphere and the skies?

Transformation and Gentleness

Just as single individuals change parts of their ordinary life after working on themselves, large groups also evolve through changes in their subgroups after large-group work. Group process work is like a tribal ritual, which becomes integrated in the following days through the gossip, reconsideration, wonderment, anger, and overall renewed interest in community life.

The next group process meeting was the first one in which the upper management took part. By this time the Esalen community had already changed. In between the large-group processes we gave seminars for the staff much like the one described in the first part of this book. We also worked with the little groups at Esalen, circles of 5 to 50 people, which had long attempted to process their community experiences together. We were amazed at the flexibility and learning capacity of the management, body workers, residential students (or work scholars), and especially the group of kitchen workers.

The final group process was the opposite of the first one. The tension was gone and the only issue that arose at that moment was a touching question about how to connect with community members who still felt excluded. We encouraged those who had not yet spoken, the "outsiders" in the room, to form a circle inside the rest. There was a coming together as our stay at Esalen drew to a close.

The Esalen family, like other little worlds, projected some of its own leadership powers on their management and visiting teachers. They could not trust that they were more capable than anyone else of healing their own wounds. Though Esalen has its own individual nature, it is a model of any place, of everyone and everywhere. We all suffer from a plurality of voices, from the conflict of having so many different belief systems. Members of all organizations, countries, communities, you and I are forever imagining that others have the intelligence, insight and power to save us, to save our planet, to be neutral and fair. All groups have this tendency to want a powerful leader or savior, and thus repress their own innate powers.

We remember our last work done at Esalen. We were experimenting with process work in a workshop called "The Living Tao." We were delighted that the T'ai Chi master, Al Huang, joined us for that seminar. (He told us that his own organization was called The Living Tao. We found that most appropriate!) The format of the seminar was determined by chance. We decided to spin a bottle; whoever it pointed to would become the object of our focus, our work for the moment, and whatever happened would be nature's recommendation for what we all needed to learn.

The bottle chose a very shy man, whom we'll call Joe. Joe must have been the shyest person at Esalen. As the bottle pointed directly at him, he began to cry. He was terrified to come out and do something in the middle. "What can I do?" he asked. "I'm too shy."

Arny asked Joe to stand up and let whatever motions were in his muscles and limbs and bones show us the way. Joe began to move his arms very slowly, and Arny gently followed Joe's movements. Joe's arms began to sway back and forth, and as Arny helped Joe pick up on this movement, it looked like he was waving a magic wand or choreographing a dance. Arny amplified this movement, and Joe started to choreograph Arny as the two of them danced and spun around together.

Joe was amazed. "I never thought I could have done this," he murmured tearfully. Arny came closer to Joe and shyly touched him and then retreated, to encourage the dance to unfold and create what wanted to happen. Joe spun around a few more times, turning to his own inner rhythm, and the rest cheered as the dance came to an end.

Al Huang stepped forward to the center of the room and warmly embraced Joe. Arny looked in from the outside and then joined them, creating a threefold embrace. Then, silently, the others joined in spontaneously until everyone in the room found themselves in an authentic community embrace with Joe and Al at the center.

The Tao spoke to us through Joe. His sensitivity created a powerful experience of being centered in the community, a feeling that had been trying to come out since the beginning of our residency there.

Unanswered Questions

We were grateful for the opportunity to help Esalen, but Esalen, too, was a magnificent teacher for us. We were able to rediscover our thesis that processing group tension rapidly leads to community creation. And in giving us the unusual opportunity to help it, Esalen allowed us to assist the very ground, buildings and infrastructure that enables seminars like the one described in this book to exist. Esalen was for us what Big Sur is for Esalen, an earth to grow on.

Now we realize that helping the ground that supports us is not only a privilege, but an obligation. If what we are doing is useful, the world around us will sense this and also ask for help, thereby transforming therapy into some new kind of politics or ecology.

At Esalen we also realized, perhaps for the first time, that organizational work cannot be taught as a group of skills, because it depends upon our own inner development. In the beginning we were indistinguishable parts of Esalen's turmoil. We were constantly drawn off on a tangent, swimming in the muddle of whether we were good or bad. We were propelled between moments of frustration and love for the groups we were working with.

Beyond all of this, Esalen challenged us to grow, in the same way it had challenged others before us. By giving us an overview of many organizational and individual therapists, political, and religious teachers, it challenged us to ask ourselves questions for which we have no answers: who are we and what are the implications of what we are doing?

PART V

Spiritual Dimensions

CHAPTER 13

The Future of Therapy

A few months after our five-week stay at Esalen, we were pondering some of the larger questions that emerged from this book. We wrote the following chapter from our discussions about our work and our seminars at Esalen.

Our present work, our doubts and passions, must imply something about the nature of therapy. But what? All of us involved in the helping professions are struggling these days with changing ideas about medicine and psychology. Our interest in transpersonal issues awakens us to the feeling of confinement by our present work, but it also disturbs us if it does not succeed in working with everyday people and problems. How do we ground our loftiest ideals in modern practice?

Changes in how we live together on this earth create changes in therapy as well. Tribal life and its shamanistic rituals are dying off in the Third World, yet in the West we are witnessing the revival of interest in the healing arts. This revival has the potential to unify those aspects of our life that are divided up by our present methods: art, music, dance, drama, and, above all, altered states of trance, ecstasy, wonder, and rage. The ancient rituals and methods contain just that mixture of politics, spiritual healing, music and art we all are so genuinely seeking.

We guess that our interest in mixing and using elements of transpersonal, Jungian, neo-Freudian, Gestalt, bodywork, dance, healing, and shamanistic methods hints at a new therapeutic form. Indeed, we suspect that many of us are already ahead of our times, for we are quietly practicing new forms of therapy without waiting for them to be named. Individual practitioners have always been more advanced than the theories they are following; our work is frequently more comprehensive than we bother to formulate.

Yet a "new" form also creates doubt in our minds: we wonder if it won't be just another of the old rational and reductionist methods. The older forms, especially Buddhist and Taoist ideas, are compellingly attractive because they stress simplicity, flow, awareness, and the emptiness aspect of being human. Any new or updated form or work must at least promise to connect us to this ancient Eastern ideal for the sake of stability and depth, and to liberate us in our encounters with today's problems of overpopulation, terrorism, racism, gang wars, drugs, AIDS, and violence.

New or Old Forms?

The old or new forms must include the Taoist *wu wei,* or "not doing," to satisfy our need to relax and have a good time. But they must also include the Zen awakening, that is, living electrically alone with ourselves and with others on the streets. A new form should instruct us to follow ourselves in meditation and acknowledge our passion for concentration and attention to "mindfulness." Yet it must not detach us in a neurotic way and decrease our responsibility for working with worldly events such as global oil spills, comatose patients, drug, and street problems, and violent economic and racial conflicts.

Expanding our idea of therapy is important, but doing so and still calling it "therapy" might be like putting old wine in a new bottle; it is no longer completely satisfying. Yet therapy must remain an important part of the work, because many people need it. All of us need help at least some of the time. But therapy is outmoded because few therapists care to be helpful all the time! This is why so many get burned out, leaving a profession in need of transformation.

Perhaps the term "spiritual" is better than therapy since it includes all of our loftiest goals. But "spiritualism" alienates those burned by religious battles, just as it excites those reaching for the stars and inflates some looking for a free ticket to nirvana.

Investigating the Dharma

Perhaps it is science. After all, research, experimentation, rigorous study, and training are important in working with others. In fact, process work is generated, in part, by something like the scientific method, a mixture of working, checking what did not work, and asking, "What on earth is going on?" Let's look at evidence from videotape work, develop new methods, expand our theories, get rejected by negative feedback from clients or trainees about new approaches, and finally change and settle for the moment with something that works.

Can a new method respect information theory in physics and still work with poltergeists and other ghosts? Will it incorporate the inquisitiveness of the beginner's mind and risk new adventures like the warrior? Can we use modern medicine and the newest psychopharmica and still be part shaman? And will our work also allow or even encourage us to have fun? Enjoying, loving, fooling around, and being in rapture are as important to us as being serious while working. We need a "work" that demands from us nothing less than complete access to all our parts and selves. Nothing else is satisfying!

We call this combination of approaches process work for lack of a better term, because "process" implies that theory and practice are in transition and can never be completed.

Learning

The process idea is very close to Buddhism. To learn equanimity, we will have to train ourselves to be awake and to concentrate even in the midst of altered states such as those that occur in ecstasy or in battle. Some of us will have to learn again how to enjoy living. We all want to laugh, but laughing enthusiastically requires not only detachment, but also awareness of how the unpredictable hides behind appearances. Alas, there is no way around learning to notice the apparent or primary events and to catch the trickster, the secondary ones!

Picking up these processes and working with them requires mindfulness, equanimity, rapture, and compassion. Compassion implies a softened heart. In process work this heart grows warm from experiencing so many dramatic events and altered states, and from realizing the immense and total potential we all have at our disposal. And compassion shows itself by opening up to the impossible, the absurd, the horrific, and the intense, even while the rest of our feelings balk in shock. The open heart says, more than anything else, "Go on, ride the horse backwards. Let the impossible unfold. Give it a democratic chance along with all the other events to unfold and become itself."

Just as transpersonal traditions frequently place little importance upon the "ego," process work has no personality theory, no higher or lower states. There are no types, no parts we hold onto—except the tendency to develop awareness; no identities that are unchanging—except, of course, the fair observer and the meta-communicator.

Rather than place the emphasis on our present or future identities, dream images, fairy-tale figures, and problems, why not place it on our constantly changing eternal nature, which has its own innate foundations in awareness? Why develop and then hold on to personality theories that describe parts or dream figures that were real only in the moment we experienced them? After all, these figures and parts always turn out to be temporarily valid; they are the names of energetic states before they transformed through unfolding.

Time Spirits and "Right Understanding"

Perhaps we should find new names for old forms, such as "childhood," "mother," and "complex," since penetrating and unfolding their messages through mindfully entering their energies transforms them. Let's invent a more flowing name for these parts: perhaps we should call them "spirits of the times" or even "time spirits."

Let's develop our way of working with change. Hold on to self-descriptions and images as long as they are valid, remembering that in essence they are some sort of time spirit. We are especially attracted by the teachings of Thich Nhat Hanh, who says that "right understanding" comes from being in the stream, while previous "knowledge" acts like an "obstacle" to it. We must all be on the same Buddhist track, which stresses the importance of transcending our previous knowledge, even knowledge of ourselves.

Cross-cultural Paradigms

We love to ponder these questions, to doubt and wonder about what we are doing. And we love unusual feedback! We were surprised to hear our seminar participants from Africa and India trying to convince us that process work had its roots in their cultures. Even a Masai medicine man we met during a safari in Kenya gave me his staff because he felt we were doing the same work. We think these Indians and Africans are trying to teach us that mindfulness, calm, compassion, and tolerance are cross-cultural, general human necessities. They are fundamental constituents of a work that attempts to deal with all situations, with everything that crosses the observer's mind and path.

Riding the Horse Backwards

The idea of riding the horse backwards reorganizes and applies ancient and cross-cultural beliefs, paradigms, skills and metaskills in such a way that we delight in finding solutions where we agreed never to look. As an example, take our ecological mess. If we ride the horse backwards, we would guess that we buy more cars, use more gas, spill more oil, and produce more children than we need because we want to asphyxiate ourselves in a global fog. And we would also guess that this is the right direction, even if it is with the wrong means.

Let's try riding forwards while reversing our viewpoint and consider the following. Why wait until we die to die? Why not drop ourselves and our present ways now: STOP THE WORLD! Everyone can choose what should stop in their own way. But certainly the vast majority of us need to "stop" our attachment to being who we think we are: sweet or nasty, ambitious or religious, cosmopolitan or materialistic! We need to be real in the sense of temporarily identifying with what we are doing and feeling at a given moment. And then we need to step out, observe and let life unfold by disidentifying with our acts. If we are ruining the world, then we need to pick it up and find the wisdom in it. Perhaps it's an attempt to commit metaphorical suicide.

Working with the unintended and unexpected is not just a paradoxical intervention in horseback riding; it is a philosophy and lifestyle that work when other solutions do not, when telling ourselves and others to stop our addictions doesn't work. With this paradigm, everyone wins, whether they live or die.

Learning Process Work

Who can do process work? Must you train in meditation, psychiatry, dream and body work, group work, relationship and movement work, shamanism, healing, dying and spiritual development? We don't think so.

Of course, process work is partially a group of techniques that can be learned, but it is mostly maintaining attitudes of concentration and awareness. If you have these, you automatically generate the tools you need in a given situation and can transform crises into festivals. But the use of these attitudes will always be a matter of personal development; they cannot simply be learned.

We are uncertain about how to teach this development. How do you grow to the point where you remain balanced in the midst of attacks or where you even look forward to their challenge? How do we develop detachment and compassion? Everything, even death, seems to point to the need for these attitudes, but who can maintain them for more than a moment? Some teachers instruct us in these feelings and skills through modeling them. Many therapists teach equanimity, mindfulness, compassion, and rapture by the way they deal with a client's worst problems. The best instructors realize that they can only point the way; the learner must do the rest.

Most learners can, or, perhaps, even must, read about the Mystery Schools of modern and ancient times, study Buddhism,

Taoism, shamanism, and the martial arts. But frankly, we think that the impossible challenges of life are the best teachers.

To learn detachment you must do what you normally do! Fight life as much as possible. Try to control it, push the river, be as "bad" and as egotistical, ambitious and tough as possible. Fight fate! HOLD ON TO EVERYTHING! At least until it wrenches itself free from you. This is process-oriented learning; accepting and going through each stage as it comes up and reaching your goal without ever knowing how you got there.

Perhaps you can't learn the "new" work, except through awareness—and then only for a moment. But notice how you forget it again, how you try, but fail to understand it, how you want to be wise and interpret, how you want to change and master the world. And finally, or rather, once again, when all else fails, realize that life itself teaches process-oriented thinking by wearing out all the other survival methods. After all, who is ready to change before exhaustion? Only when we are at the end of the line, are some of us, some of the time, ready to open up and ride the horse backwards.

In this singular, if temporary, moment a kind of awesome peace arises from the turbulence of life, even as the storm goes on. And we remember that this quiet spot was there all the time, waiting for us to enter, hidden in the midst of individual and social change.

Bibliography

Dennehy, Virginia, "Process-Oriented Body Work and Religious Experience." Unpublished Ph.D. dissertation, Palo Alto, California, Institute for Transpersonal Psychology, 1988.

Diamond, Julie, "Patterns of Communication." Unpublished manuscript, Zurich, 1988. Available through Lao Tse Press.

Goodbread, Joseph, *The Dreambody Toolkit*. Lao Tse Press, 1997.

Hanh, Thich Nhat, *The Heart of Understanding*. Berkeley, Calif., Parallax Press, 1988.

Mindell, Amy (formerly Amy Kaplan), "The Hidden Dance: Introduction to Process-Oriented Movement Work." Unpublished Master's thesis, Yellow Springs, Ohio, Antioch University, 1986.

Mindell, Amy, *Metaskills: The Spiritual Art of Therapy*. Tempe, Arizona, New Falcon Publications, 1995.

Mindell, Amy, "Moon in the Water: The Metaskills of Process-Oriented Psychology." Unpublished Ph.D. dissertation, Cincinnati, Union Institute, 1991.

Mindell, Arnold, *City Shadows*. Harmondsworth, Penguin Arkana, 1988.

Mindell, Arnold, *Coma: Key to Awakening*. Boston, Mass., Shambhala, 1989.

Mindell, Arnold, *Dreambody*. Boston, Mass., Sigo Press, 1982; Harmondsworth, Penguin Arkana, 1988; Lao Tse Press, 1998.

Mindell, Arnold, *The Dreambody in Relationships*. Harmondsworth, Penguin Arkana, 1987; Lao Tse Press, 2002.

Mindell, Arnold, *River's Way.* Harmondsworth, Penguin Arkana, 1988. Arkana, 1985.

Mindell, Arnold, *Working on Yourself Alone.* Harmondsworth, Penguin Arkana, 1990; Lao Tse Press, 2002.

Mindell, Arnold, *Working with the Dreaming Body.* Harmondsworth, Penguin; Lao Tse Press, 2002.

Mindell, Arnold, *The Year I: Global Process Work.* Harmondsworth, Penguin Arkana, 1989.

Video Tapes

Mindell, Arnold:

Conflict Resolution. Process Work Center of Portland, 2049 NW Hoyt St., Portland, OR 97209 USA.

Process-Oriented Psychology. Thinking Allowed, National Public TV Broadcast, 2560 9th St., Suite 123 Berkeley CA 94710, USA. Mindell, Amy and Arnold,

Working with the Dying. Thinking Allowed Productions, National TV Broadcast, 2560 9th St., Suite 123 Berkeley CA 94710, USA.

Mindell, Amy and Arnold:

Illness and Life Myth: Chronic Symptoms. A TV program of 4 evenings, Lao Tse Press, Ltd., P.O. Box 8898 Portland, OR 97207 USA.

Process Works. A TV program of 3 evenings, Lao Tse Press, Ltd., P.O. Box 8898 Portland, OR 97207 USA.